Privy Seal: His

Ford Madox Ford

Alpha Editions

This edition published in 2024

ISBN 9789362518231

Design and Setting By
Alpha Editions
www.alphaedis.com
Email - info@alphaedis.com

Contents

PART ONE
THE RISING SUN

I

The Magister Udal sat in the room of his inn in Paris, where customarily the King of France lodged such envoys as came at his expense. He had been sent there to Latinise the letters that passed between Sir Thomas Wyatt and the King's Ministers of France, for he was esteemed the most learned man in these islands. He had groaned much at being sent there, for he must leave in England so many loves—the great, blonde Margot Poins, that was maid to Katharine Howard; the tall, swaying Katharine Howard herself; Judge Cantre's wife that had fed him well; and two other women, with all of whom he had succeeded easily or succeeded in no wise at all. But the mission was so well paid—with as many crowns the day as he had had groats for teaching the Lady Mary of England—that fain he had been to go. Moreover, it was by way of being a favour of Privy Seal's. The magister had written for him a play in English; the rich post was the reward—and it was an ill thing, a thing the magister dreaded, to refuse the favours of Privy Seal. He consoled himself with the thought that the writing of letters in Latin might wash from his mouth the savour of the play he had written in the vulgar tongue.

But his work in Paris was ended—for with the flight of Cardinal Pole, who had left Paris precipitately upon news that the King of England had sent a drunken roisterer to assassinate him, it was imagined that soon now more concord between Francis and England might ensue, and the magister sat in his room planning his voyage back to Dover. The room was great in size, panelled mostly in wood, lit with lampwicks that floated in oil dishes and heated with a sea-coal fire, for though it was April the magister was of a cold disposition of the hands and shins. The inn—of the Golden Astrolabe—was kept by an Englishwoman, a masterful widow with a broad face and a great mouth that smiled. She stood beside him there. Forty-seven she might have been, and she called herself the Widow Annot.

The magister sat over his fire with his gown parted from his legs to warm his shins, but his hands waved angrily and his face was crestfallen.

'Oh, keeper of a tavern,' he said. 'It is set down in holy writ that it is not good for a man to be alone.'

'That a hostess shall keep her tavern clean is writ in the books of the provost of Paris town,' the Widow Annot answered, and the shadow of her great white hood, which she wore in the older English fashion, danced over the brown wooden beams of the ceiling.

'Nay, nay,' he answered, 'it is written there that it is the enjoined devoir of every hotelier to provide things fitting for the sojourners' ease, pleasure and recreation.'

'The maid is locked in another house,' the hostess answered, 'and should have been this three week.' She swung her keys on a black riband and gazed at him masterfully. 'Will your magistership eat capon or young goat?'

'Capon will have a savour like sawdust, and young goat like the dust of the road,' the magister moaned. 'Give me the girl to wait upon me again.'

'No maid will wait upon thee,' she answered.

'Even thou thyself?' he asked. He glanced across his shoulder and his eyes measured her, hers him. She had large shoulders, a high, full stomacher, and her cheeks were an apple-red. 'The maiden was a fair piece,' he tittered.

'Therefore you must spoil the ring of the coin,' she answered.

He sighed: 'Then eat you with me. "*Soli cantare periti Arcades.*" But it is cold here alone of nights.'

They ate goat and green leeks sweetened with honey, and wood thrushes pickled in wine, and salt fish from the mouth of the Beauce. And because this gave the magister a great thirst he drank much of a warmed wine from Burgundy that the hostess brought herself. They sat, byside, on cushions on a couch before the warm fire.

'*Filia pulchra mater pulchrior!*' the magister muttered, and he cast his arms about her soft and plump waist. 'The maid was a fair skewer, the hostess is a plumper roasting bit.' She took his kisses on her fire-warmed cheeks, but in the end she thrust him mightily from her with a large elbow.

He gasped with the strength of her thrust, and she said:

'Greedy dogs getten them hard cuffs,' and rearranged her neckercher. When he tried to come nearer her she laughed and thrust him aback.

'You have tried and tasted,' she said. 'A fuller meal you must pay for.'

He stood before her, lean and lank, his gown flapping about his calves, his eyes smiling humorously, his lips twitching.

'Oh soft and warm woman,' he cried, 'payment shall be yours'; and whilst he fumbled furiously in his clothes-press, he quoted from Tully: '*Haec civitas mulieri redimiculum praebuit.*' He pulled out one small bag: '*Haec in collum.*' She took another. '*Haec in crines!*' and he added a third, saying: 'Here is all I have,' and cast the three into her lap. Whilst she counted the coins composedly on the table before her he added: 'Leave me nevertheless the price to come to England with.'

'Sir Magister,' she said, turning her large face to him. 'This is not one-tenth enough. You have tasted an ensample. Will you have the whole meal?'

'Oh, unconscionable,' he cried. 'More I have not!' He began to wave his hands. 'Consider what you do do,' he uttered. 'Think of what a pest is love. How many have died of it. Pyramus, Thisbe, Dido, Medea, Croesus, Callirhoe, Theagines the philosopher ... Consider what writes Gordonius: "*Prognosticatio est talis: si non succuratur iis aut in maniam cadunt: aut moriuntur.*" Unless lovers be succoured either they fall into a madness, either they die or grow mad. And Fabian Montaltus: "If this passion be not assuaged, the inflammation cometh to the brain. It drieth up the blood. Then followeth madness or men make themselves away." I would have you ponder of what saith Parthenium and what Plutarch in his tales of lovers.'

Her face appeared comely and smooth in his eyes, but she shook her head at him.

'These be woeful and pretty stories,' she said. 'I would have you to tell me many of them.'

'All through the night,' he said eagerly, and made to clasp her in his arms. But she pushed him back again with her hand on his chest.

'All through the night an you will,' she said. 'But first you shall tell a prettier tale before a man in a frock.'

He sprang full four feet back at one spring.

'I have wedded no woman, yet,' he said.

'Then it is time you wed one now,' she answered.

'Oh widow, bethink you,' he pleaded. 'Would you spoil so pretty a tale? Would you humble so goodly a man's pride?'

'Why, it were a pity,' she said. 'But I am minded to take a husband.'

'You have done well this ten years without one,' he cried out.

Her face seemed to set like adamant as she turned her cheek to him.

'Call it a woman's mad freak,' she said.

'Six and twenty pupils in the fair game of love I have had,' he said. 'You shall be the seven and twentieth. Twenty and seven are seven and two. Seven and two are nine. Now nine is the luckiest of numbers. Be you that one.'

'Nay,' she answered. 'It is time you learned husbandry who have taught so many and earned so little.'

He slipped himself softly into the cushions beside her.

'Would you spoil so fair a tale?' he said. 'Would you have me to break so many vows? I have promised a mort of women marriage, and so long as I be not wed I may keep faith with any one of them.'

She held her face away from him and laughed.

'That is as it may be,' she said. 'But when you wed with me to-night you will keep faith with one woman.'

'Woman,' he pleaded. 'I am a great scholar.'

'Ay,' she answered, 'and great scholars have climbed to great estates.'

She continued to count the coins that came from his little money-bags; the shadow of her hood upon the great beams grew more portentous.

'It is thought that your magistership may rise to be Chancellor of the Realm of England,' she added.

He clutched his forehead.

'Eheu!' he said. 'If you have heard men say that, you know that wedded to thee I could never climb.'

'Then I shall very comfortably keep my inn here in Paris town,' she answered. 'You have here fourteen pounds and eleven shillings.'

He stretched forth his lean hands:

'Why, I will marry thee in the morning,' he said, and he moistened his lips with the tip of his tongue. Outside the door there was a shuffling of several feet.

'I knew not other guests were in the house,' he uttered, and fell again to kissing her.

'Knew you not an envoy was come from Cleves?' she whispered.

Her head fell back and he supported it with one trembling hand. He shook like a leaf when her voice rang out:

'*Au secours! Au secours!*

There was a great jangle, light fell into the dusky room through the doorhole, and he found himself beneath the eyes of many scullions with spits, cooks with carving forks, and kitchenmaids with sharpened distaffs of steel.

'Now I will be wed this night,' she laughed.

He moved to the end of the couch and blinked at her in the strong light.

'I will be wed this night,' she said again, and rearranged her head-dress, revealing, as her sleeves fell open, her white, plump arms.

'Why, no!' he answered irresolutely.

She said in French to her aids:

'Come near him with the spits!'

They moved towards him, a white-clad body with their pointed things glittering in the light of torches. He sprang behind the great table against the window and seized the heavy-leaden sandarach. The French scullions knew, tho' he had no French, that he would cleave one of their skulls, and they stood, a knot of seven—four men and three maids—in blue hoods, in the centre of the room.

'By Mars and by Apollo!' he said, 'I was minded to wed with thee if I could no other way. But now, like Phaeton, I will cast myself from the window and die, or like the wretches thrown from the rock, called Tarpeian. I was minded to a folly: now I am minded rather for death.'

'How nobly thy tongue doth wag, husband,' she said, and cried in French for the rogues to be gone. When the door closed upon the lights she said in the comfortable gloom: 'I dote upon thy words. My first was tongue-tied.' She beckoned him to her and folded her arms. 'Let us discourse upon this matter,' she said comfortably. 'Thus I will put it: you wed with me or spring from the window.'

'I am even trapped?' he asked.

'So it comes to all foxes that too long seek for capons,' she answered.

'But consider,' he said. He sat himself by the fireside upon a stool, being minded to avoid temptation.

'I would have your magistership forget the rogues that be without,' she said.

'They were a nightmare's tale,' he said.

'Yet forget them not too utterly,' she answered. 'For I am of some birth. My father had seven horses and never followed the plough.'

'Oh buxom one!' he answered. 'Of a comfortable birth and girth thou art. Yet with thee around my neck I might not easily climb.'

'Magister,' she said, 'whilst thou climbest in London town thy wife will bide in Paris.'

'Consider!' he said. 'There is in London town a fair, large maid called Margot Poins.'

'Is she more fair than I?' she asked. 'I will swear she is.'

He tilted his stool forward.

'No; no, I swear it,' he said eagerly.

'Then I will swear she is more large.'

'No; not one half so bounteous is her form,' he answered, and moved across to the couch.

'Then if you can bear her weight up you can bear mine,' she said, and moved away from him.

'Nay,' he answered. 'She would help me on,' and he fumbled in the shadows for her hand. She drew herself together into a small space.

'You affect her more than me,' she said, with a swift motion simulating jealousy.

'By the breasts of Venus, no!' he answered.

'Oh, once more use such words,' she murmured, and surrendered to him her soft hand. He rubbed it between both of his cold ones and uttered:

'By the Paphian Queen: by her teams of doves and sparrows! By the bower of Phyllis and the girdle of Egypt's self! I love thee!'

She gurgled 'oh's' of pleasure.

'But this Margot Poins is tirewoman to the Lady Katharine Howard.'

'I am tirewoman to mine own self alone,' she said. 'Therefore you love her better.'

'Nay, oh nay,' he said gently. 'But this Lady Katharine Howard is mistress to the King's self.'

'And I have been mistress to no married man save my husbands,' she answered. 'Therefore you love this Margot Poins better.'

He fingered her soft palm and rubbed it across his own neck.

'Nay, nay,' he said. 'But I must wed with Margot Poins.'

'Why with her more than with me or any other of your score and seven?' she said softly.

'Since the Lady Katharine will be Queen,' he answered, and once again he was close against her side. She sighed softly.

'Thus if you wed with me you will never be Chancellor,' she said.

'I would not anger the Queen,' he answered. She nestled bountifully and warmly against him.

'Swear even again that you like me more than the fair, large wench in London town,' she whispered against his ear.

'Even as Jove prized Danaë above the Queen of Heaven, even as Narcissus prized his shadow above all the nymphs, even as Hercules placed Omphale above his strength, or even as David the King of the Jews Bathsheba above....'

She murmured 'Oh, oh,' and placed her arms around his shoulders.

'How I love thy brave words!'

'And being Chancellor,' he swore, 'I will come back to thee, oh woman of the sweet smiles, honey of Hymettus, Cypriote wine....'

She moved herself a little from him in the darkness.

'And if you do not wed with Margot Poins....'

'I pray a plague may fall upon her, but I must wed with her,' he answered. 'Come now; come now!'

'Else the Lady Katharine shall be displeased with your magistership?'

He sought to draw her to him, but she stiffened herself a little.

'And this Lady Katharine is mistress to the King of England's realm?'

His hands moved tremblingly towards her in the darkness.

'And this Lady Katharine shall be Queen?'

A hiss of exasperation came upon his lips, for she had slipped from beneath his hands into the darkness.

'Why, then, I will not stay your climbing,' she said. 'Good-night,' and in the darkness he heard her sob.

The couch fell backwards as he swore and sprang towards her voice.

'Magister!' she said. 'Hands off! Unwed thou shalt not have me, for I have sworn it.'

'I have sworn to wed seven and twenty women,' he said, 'and have wedded with none.'

'Nay, nay,' she sobbed. 'Hands off. Henceforth I will make no vows—but no one but thee shall wed me.'

'Then wed me, in God's name!' he cried, and, screaming:

'*Ho là! Apportez le prestre!*' she softened herself in his arms.

The magister confronted the lights, the leering scullions and the grinning maids with their great mantles; his brown, woodpecker-like face was alike crestfallen and thirsty with desire. A lean Dominican, with his brown cowl back and spectacles of horn, gabbled over his missal and took a crown's fee—then asked another by way of penitence for the sin with the maid locked up in another house. When they brought the bride favours of pink to pin into her gorget she said:

'I long had loved thee for thy great words, husband. Therefore all these I had in readiness.'

With that knot fast upon him, the magister, clasping his gown upon his shins, looked askance at the floor. Whilst they made ready the bride, with great lights and laughter, she said:

'I was minded to have a comfortable husband. And a comfortable husband is a husband much absent. What more comfortable than me in Paris town and thee in London city? I keep my inn here, thou mindest thy book there. Thou shalt here find a goodly capon upon occasion, and when thou hast a better house in London I will come share it.'

'Trapped! Trapped!' the magister muttered to himself. 'Even as was Sir Launcelot!'

He considered of the fair and resentful Margot Poins whom it was incumbent indeed that he should wed: that Katharine Howard loved her well and was in these matters strait-laced. When his eyes measured his wife he licked his lips; when his eyes were on the floor his jaw fell. At best the new Mistress Udal would be in Paris. He looked at the rope tied round the thin middle of the brown priest, and suddenly he leered and cast off his cloak.

'Let me remember to keep an equal mind in these hard matters,' he quoted, and fell to laughing.

For he remembered that in England no marriage by a friar or monk held good in those years. Therefore he was the winner. And the long, square room, with the cave bed behind its shutter in the hollow of the wall, the light-coloured, square beams, and the foaming basin of bride-ale that a fat-armed girl in a blue kerseymere gown served out to scullion after scullion; the open windows from which a little knave was casting bride-pennies to some screaming beggars and women in the street; the blind hornman whose unseeing eyes glanced along the reed of his bassoon that he played before the open door; the two saucy maids striving to wrest the bride's stockings one from the other—all these things appeared friendly and jovial in his eyes. So that, when one of the maids, wresting the stocking, fell hard against him, he clasped her in his arms and kissed her till she struggled from him to drink a mug of bride-ale.

'*Hodie mihi: mihi atque cras!*' he said. For it was in his mind a goodly thing to pay a usuress with base coins.

II

It was three days later, in the morning, that his captress said to the Magister Udal:

'Husband, it is time that I gave thee the bridal gift.'

The magister, happy with a bellyful of carp, bread and breakfast ale, muttered 'Anan?' from above his copy of Lucretius. He sat in the window-seat of the great stone kitchen. Upon one long iron spit before the fire fourteen trussed capons turned in unison; the wooden shoes of the basting-maid clattered industriously; and from the chimney came the clank of the invisible smoke-vanes and the be-sooted chains. The magister, who loved above all things warmth, a full stomach, a comfortable woman and a good book, had all these things; he was well minded to stay in Paris town for fourteen days, when they were to slay a brown pig from the Ardennes, against whose death he had written an elegy in Sapphics.

'For,' said his better half, standing before him with a great loaf clasped to her bosom, 'if you turn a horse from the stable between full and half full, like as not he will return of fair will to the crib.'

'Oh Venus and Hebe in one body,' the magister said, 'I am minded to end here my scholarly days.'

'I am minded that ye shall travel far erstwhile,' she answered.

He laid down his book upon a clean chopping-board.

'I know a good harbourage,' he said.

She sat down beside him in the window and fingered the fur on his long gown, saying that, in this light, it showed ill-favouredly worm-eaten; and he answered that he never had wishes nor money for gowning himself, who cultivated the muses upon short commons. She turned rightway to the front the medal upon his chest, and folded her arms.

'Whilst ye have no better house to harbour us,' she said, 'this shall serve. Let us talk of the to-come.'

He groaned a little.

'Let us love to-day that's here,' he said. 'I will read thee a verse from Lucretius, and you shall tell me the history of that fourth capon'—he pointed to a browned carcase that, upon the spit, whirled its elbows a full third longer than any of the line.

'That is the master roasting-piece,' she said, 'so he browns there not too far, nor too close, for the envoy's own eating.'

He considered the chicken with his head to one side.

'It is the place of a wife to be subject to her lord,' he said.

'It is the place of a husband that he fendeth for 's wife,' she answered him. She tapped her fingers determinedly upon her elbows.

'So it is,' she continued. 'To-morrow you shall set out for London city to make road towards becoming Sir Chancellor.' Whilst he groaned she laid down for him her law. He was to go to England, he was to strive for great posts: if he gained, she would come share them; if he failed, he might at odd moments come back to her fireside. 'Have done with groaning now,' she said, stilling his lamentations.' 'Keep them even for the next wench that you shall sue to—of me you have had all you asked.'

He considered for five seconds, his elbow upon his crossed knees and his wrist supporting his lean brown face.

'It is in the essence of it a good bargain,' he said. 'You put against the chance of being, you a chancellor's madam, mine of having for certain a capon in Paris town.'

He tapped his long nose. 'Nevertheless, for your stake you have cast down a very little: three nights of bed and board against the chaining me up.'

'Husband,' she answered. 'More than that you shall have.'

He wriggled a little beneath his furs.

'Husband is an ill name,'he commented. 'It smarts.'

'But it fills the belly.'

'Aye,'he said. 'Therefore I am minded to bide here and take with the sourness the sweet of it.'

She laughed a little, and, with a great knife, cut a large manchet from the loaf between them.

'Nay,' she said, 'to-morrow my army with their spits and forks shall drive thee from the door.'

He grinned with his lips. She was fair and fat beneath her hood, but she was resolute. 'I have it in me greatly to advance you,' she said.

A boy brought her a trencher filled with chopped things, and a man in a blue jerkin came to her side bearing a middling pig, seared to a pale clear pinkness. The boy held the slit stomach carefully apart, and she lined it with slices of bread, dropping into the hollow chives, nutmegs, lumps of salt, the buds of bergamot, and marigold seeds with their acrid perfume, and balls of honied suet. She bound round it a fair linen cloth that she stitched with a great bone needle.

'Oh ingenuous countenance,' the magister mused above the pig's mild face. 'Is it not even the spit of the Cleves envoy's? And the Cleves envoy shall eat this adorable monster. Oh, cruel anthropophagist!'

She resigned her burden to the spit and gave the loaf to the boy, wiped her fingers upon her apron, and said:

'That pig shall help thee far upon thy road.'

'Goes it into my wallet?' he asked joyfully.

She answered: 'Nay; into the Cleves envoy's weam.'

'You speak in hard riddles,' he uttered.

'Nay,' she laughed, 'a baby could unriddle it.' She looked at him for a moment to enjoy her triumph of mystery. 'Husband mine, a pig thus stuffed is good eating for Cleves men. I have not kept a hostel for twelve years for envoys and secretaries without learning what each eats with pleasure. And long have I thought that if I wed a man it should be such a man as could thrive by learning of envoys' secrets.'

He leaned towards her earnestly.

'You know wherefore the man from Cleves is come?'

'You are, even as I have heard it said, a spy of Thomas Cromwell?' she asked in return.

He looked suddenly abashed, but she held to her question.

'I pass for Privy Seal's man,' he answered at last.

'But you have played him false,' she said. He grew pale, glanced over his shoulder, and put his finger on his lips.

'I'll wager it was for a woman,' she accused him. She wiped her lips with her apron and dropped her hands upon her lap.

'Why, keep troth to Cromwell if you can,' she said.

'I do think his sun sets,' he whispered.

'Why, I am sorry for it,' she answered. 'I have always loved him for a brewer's son. My father was a brewer.'

'Cromwell was begotten even by the devil,' Udal answered. 'He made me write a comedy in the vulgar tongue.'

'Be it as you will,' she answered. 'You shall know on which side to bite your cake better than I.'

He was still a little shaken at the thought of Privy Seal.

'If you know wherefore cometh Cleves' envoy, much it shall help me to share the knowledge,' he said at last, 'for by that I may know whether Cromwell or we do rise or fall.'

'If you have made a pact with a woman, have very great cares,' she answered dispassionately. 'Doubtless you know how the dog wags its tail; but you are always a fool with a woman.'

'This woman shall be Queen if Cromwell fall,' the magister said, 'and I shall rise with her.'

'But is no woman from Cleves' Queen there now?' she asked.

'Cicely,' he answered highly, 'you know much of capons and beeves, but there are queens that are none and do not queen it, and queans that are no queens and queen it.'

'And so 'twill be whilst men are men,' she retorted. 'But neither my first nor my second had his doxies ruling within my house, do what they might beyond the door.'

He tried to impart to her some of the adoration he had for Katharine Howard—her learning, her faith, her tallness, her wit, and the deserved empiry that she had over King Henry VIII; but she only answered:

'Why, kiss the wench all you will, but do not come to tell me how she smells!'—and to his new protests: 'Aye, you may well be right and she may well be Queen—for I know you will sacrifice your ease for no wench that shall not help you somewhere forwards.'

The magister held his hands above his head in shocked negation of this injustice—but there came from the street the thin wail of a trumpet; another joined it, and a third; the three sounds executed a triple convolution and died away one by one. Holding his thin hand out for silence and better hearing, he muttered:

'Norfolk's tucket! Then it is true that Norfolk comes to Paris.'

His wife slipped down from her seat.

'Gave I you not the ostler's gossip from Calais three days since?' she said, and went towards her roastings.

'But wherefore comes the yellow dog to Paris?' Udal persisted.

'That you may go seek,' she answered. 'But believe always what an innkeeper says of who are on the road.'

Udal too slipped down from the window-seat; he buttoned his gown down to his shins, pulled his hat over his ears and hurried through the galleried courtyard into the comfortless shadows of the street. There was no doubt that Norfolk was coming; round the tiny crack that, two houses away, served for all the space that the road had between the towering housefronts, two men in scarlet and yellow, with leopards and lions and fleurs-de-lis on their chests, walked between two in white, tabarded with the great lilies of France. They crushed round the corner, for there was scarce space for four men abreast; behind them squeezed men in purple with the Howard knot, bearing pikes, and men in mustard yellow with the eagle's wing and ship badge of the Provost of Paris. In the broader space before the arch of Udal's courtyard they stayed to wait for the horsemen to disentangle themselves from the alley; the Englishmen looked glumly at the tall housefronts; the French loosened the mouthplates of their helmets to breathe the air for a minute. Hostlers, packmen and pedlars began to fill the space behind Udal, and he heard his wife's voice calling shrilly to a cook who had run across the yard.

The crowd a little shielded him from the draught which came through the arch, and he waited with more contentment. Undoubtedly there was Norfolk upon a great yellow horse, so high that it made his bonnet almost touch the overhanging storey of the third house; behind him the white and gold litter of the provost, who, having three weeks before broken his leg at tennis-play, was still unable to sit in a saddle. The duke rode as if implacably rigid, his yellow, long face set, listening as if with a sour deafness to something that the provost from below called to him with a great, laughing voice.

The provost's litter, too, came up alongside the duke's horse in the open space, then they all moved forward at the slow processional: three steps and a halt for the trumpets to blow a tucket; three more and another tucket; the great yellow horse stepping high and casting up his head, from which flew many flakes of white foam. With its slow, regularly interrupted gait, dominated by the impassive yellow face of Norfolk, the whole band had an air of performing a solemn dance, and Udal shivered for a long time, till amidst the train of mules bearing leathern sacks, cupboards, chests and commodes, he saw come riding a familiar figure in a scholar's gown—the young pedagogue and companion of the Earl of Surrey. He was a fair, bearded youth with blue eyes, riding a restless colt that embroiled itself and plunged amongst the mules' legs. The young man leaned forward in the saddle and craned to avoid a clothes chest.

The magister called to him:

'Ho, Longstaffe!' and having caught his pleased eyes: *'Ecce quis sto in arce plenitatis. Veni atque bibe! Magister sum. Udal sum. Longstaffe ave.'*

Longstaffe slipped from his horse, which he left to be rescued by whom it might from amongst the hard-angled cases.

'Assuredly,' he said, 'there is no love between that beast and me as there was betwixt his lord and Bucephalus,' and he followed Udal into the galleried courtyard, where their two gowned figures alone sought shelter from the March showers.

'News from overseas there is none,' he said. 'Privy Seal ruleth still about the King; the German astronomers have put forth a tract *De Quadratura Circuli*; the lost continent of Atlantis is a lost continent still—and my bones ache.'

'But your mission?' Udal asked.

The doctor, his hard blue eyes spinning with sardonic humour beneath his black beretta, said that his mission, even as Udal's had been, was to gain some crowns by setting into the learned language letters that should pass between his ambassador and the King's men of France. Udal grinned disconcertedly.

'Be certified in your mind,' he said, 'that I am not here a spy or informer of Privy Seal's.'

'Forbid it, God,' Doctor Longstaffe answered good-humouredly. None the less his jaw hardened beneath his fair beard and he answered, 'I have as yet written no letters—*litteras nullas scripsi: argal nihil scio.*'

'Why, ye shall drink a warmed draught and eat a drippinged soppet,' Udal said, 'and you shall tell me what in England is said of this mission.'

He led the fair doctor into the great kitchen, and felt a great stab of dislike when the young man set his arm round the hostess's waist and kissed her on the red cheeks. The young man laughed:

'Aye indeed; I am *mancipium paucae lectionis* set beside so learned a man as the magister.'

The hostess received him with a bridling favour, rubbing her cheek pleasantly, whilst Udal was seeking to persuade himself that, since the woman was in law no wife of his, he had no need to fear. Nevertheless rage tore him when the doctor, leaning his back against the window-side, talked to the woman. She stood between them holding a pewter flagon of mulled hypocras upon a salver of burnished pewter.

'Who I be,' he said, gazing complacently at her, 'is a poor student of good letters; how I be here is as one of the amanuenses of the Duke of Norfolk. Origen, Eusebius telleth, had seven, given him by Ambrosius to do his behest. The duke hath but two, given him by the grace of God and of the King's high mercy.'

'I make no doubt,' she answered, 'ye be as learned as the seven were.'

'I be twice as hungry,' he laughed; 'but with me it has always been "*Quid scribam non quemadmodum*," wherein I follow Seneca.'

'Doctor,' the magister uttered, quivering, 'you shall tell me why this mission—which is a very special embassy—at this time cometh to this town of Paris.'

'Magister,' the doctor answered, wagging his beard upon his poor collar to signify that he desired to keep his neck where it was, 'I know not.'

'Injurious man,' Udal fulminated, 'I be no spy.'

The doctor surveyed his perturbation with cross-legged calmness.

'An ye were,' he said—'and it is renowned that ye are—ye could get no knowledge from where none is.'

'Why, tell me of a woman,' the hostess said. 'Who is Kat Howard?'

The doctor's blue eyes shot a hard glance at her, and he let his head sink down.

'I have copied to her eyes a sonnet or twain,' he said, 'and they were writ by my master, Surrey, the Duke o' Norfolk's son.'

'Then these rave upon her as doth the magister?' she asked.

'Why, an ye be jealous of the magister here,' the doctor clipped his words precisely, 'cast him away and take me who am a proper sweetheart.'

'I be wed,' she answered pleasantly.

'What matters that,' he said, 'when husbands are not near?'

The magister, torn between his unaccustomed gust of jealousy and the desire to hide his marriage from a disastrous discovery in England, clutched with straining fingers at his gown.

'Tell wherefore cometh your mission,' he said.

'We spoke of a fair woman,' the doctor answered. 'Shame it were before Apollo and Priapus that men's missions should come before kings' mistresses.'

'It is true, then, that she shall be queen?' Udal's wife asked.

The fall of a great dish in the rear of the tall kitchen gave the scholar time to collect his suspicions—for he took it for an easy thing that this woman, if she were Udal's leman, might be, she too, a spy in the service of Privy Seal.

'Forbid it, God,' he said, 'that ye take my words as other than allegorical. The lady Katharine may be spoken of as a king's mistress since in truth she were a fit mistress for a king, being fair, devout, learned, courteous, tall and sweet-voiced. But that she hath been kind to the King, God forbid that I should say it.'

'Aye,' Udal said, 'but if she hath sent this mission?'

Panic rose in the heart of the doctor; he beheld himself there, in what seemed a spy's kitchen, asked disastrous questions by a man and woman and pinned into a window-seat. For there was no doubt that the rumour ran in England that this mission had been sent by the King because Katharine Howard so wished it sent. In that age of spies and treacheries no man's head was safe on his shoulders—and here were Cromwell's spies asking news of Cromwell's chief enemy.

He stretched out a calm hand and spoke slowly:

'Madam hostess,' he said, 'if ye be jealous of the magister ye may well be jealous, for great beauty and worship hath this lady.' Yet she need be little jealous, for this lady was nowadays prized so high that she might marry any man in the land—and learned men were little prized. Any man in the land of England she might wed—saving only such as were wed, amongst whom was their lord the King, who was happily wed to the gracious lady whom my Lord Privy Seal did bring from Cleves to be their very virtuous Queen.

Here, it seemed to him, he had cleared himself very handsomely of suspicion of ill will to Privy Seal or of wishing ill to Anne of Cleves.

'For the rest,' he said, sighing with relief to be away from dangerous grounds, 'your magister is safe from the toils of marriage with the Lady Katharine.' Still it might be held that jealousy is aroused by the loving and not by the returning of that love; for it was very certain that the magister much had loved this lady. Many did hold it a treachery in him, till now, to the Privy Seal whom he served. But now he might love her duteously, since our lord the King had commanded the Lady Katharine to join hands with Privy Seal, and Privy Seal to cement a friendly edifice in his heart towards the lady. Thus it was no treason to Privy Seal in him to love her. But to her it was a treason great and not to be comprehended.

He ogled Udal's wife in the gallant manner and prayed her to prepare a bed for him in that hostelry. He had been minded to lodge with a Frenchman named Clement; but having seen her ...

'Learned sir,' she answered, 'a good bed I have for you.' But if he sought to go beyond her lips she had a body-guard of spitmen that the magister's self had seen.

The doctor kissed her agreeably and, with a great sigh of relief, hurried from the door.

'May Bacchus who maketh mad, and the Furies that pursued Orestes, defile the day when I cross this step again,' he muttered as he swung under the arch and ran to follow the mule train.

For the magister, by playing with his reputation of being Cromwell's spy, had so effectually caused terror of himself to pervade those who supported the old faith that he had much ado at times to find company even amongst the lovers of good letters.

III

In the kitchen the spits had ceased turning, the dishes had been borne upstairs to the envoy from Cleves, the scullions were wiping knives, the maids were rubbing pieces of bread in the dripping pans and licking their fingers after the succulent morsels. The magister stood, a long crimson blot in the window-way; the hostess was setting flagons carefully into the great armoury.

'Madam wife,' the magister said to her at last, when she came near, 'ye see how weighty it is that I bide here.'

'Husband,' she said, 'I see how weighty it is that ye hasten to London.'

His rage broke—he whirled his arms above his head.

'Naughty woman!' he screamed harshly. 'Shalt be beaten.' He strode across to the basting range and gripped a great ladle, his brown eyes glinting, and stood caressing his thin chin passionately.

She folded her arms complacently.

'Husband,' she said, 'it is well that wives be beaten when they have merited it. But, till I have, I have seven cooks and five knaves to bear my part.'

Udal's hand fell suddenly and dispiritedly to his side. What indeed could he do? He could not beat this woman unless she would be beaten—and she stood there, square, buxom, solid and composed. He had indeed that sense that all scholars must have in presence of assured wives, that she was the better man. Moreover, the rage that had filled him in presence of Doctor Longstaffe had cooled down to nothing in Longstaffe's absence.

He folded his arms and tried impatiently to think where, in this pickle, his feet had landed him. His wife turned once more to place flagons in the armoury.

'Woman,' he said at last, in a tone half of majesty, half of appeal, 'see ye not how weighty it is that I bide here?'

'Husband,' she answered with her tranquil nonchalance, 'see ye not how weighty it is that ye waste here no more days?'

'But very well you know,' and he stretched out to her a thin hand, 'that here be two embassies of mystery: you have had, these three days, the Cleves envoy in the house. You have seen that the Duke of Norfolk comes here as ambassador.'

She took a stool and sat near his feet to listen to him.

'Now,' he began again, 'if I be in truth a spy for Thomas Cromwell, Lord Privy Seal, where can I spy better for him than here? For the Cleves people are befriended with Privy Seal; then why come they to France, where bide only Privy Seal's enemies? Now Norfolk is the chiefest enemy of Privy Seal; then wherefore cometh Norfolk to this land, where abide only these foes of Privy Seal?'

She set her elbows on her knees and her knuckles below her chin, and gazed up at him like a child.

'Tell me, husband,' she said; 'be ye a true spy for Thomas Cromwell?'

He glanced round him with terror—but no man stood nearer than the meat boards across the kitchen, so far out of earshot that they could not hear feet upon the bricks.

'Nay, ye may tell me the very truth of the very truth,' she said. 'These be false days—but my kitchen gear is thine, and nothing doth so bind folks together.'

'But other listeners—' he said.

'Hosts and hostesses are listeners,' she answered. "Tis their trade. And their trade it is, too, to fend from them all other listeners. Here you may speak. Tell me then, if I may serve you, very truly whether ye be a true spy for Thomas Cromwell or against him.'

Her round face, beneath the great white hood, had a childish earnestness.

'Why, you are a fair doxy,' he said. He hung his head for some more minutes, then he spoke again.

'It is a folly to speak of me as Privy Seal's spy, though I have so spoken of myself. For why? It gaineth me worship, maketh men to fear me and women to be dazzled by my power. But in truth, I have little power.'

'That is the very truth?' she asked.

He nodded nonchalantly and waited again to find very clear words for her understanding.

'But, though it be true that I am no spy of Cromwell's, true it is also that I am a very poor man who craves very much for money. For I love good books that cost much gold; comely women that cost far more; succulent meats, sweet wines, high piled fires and warm furs.'

He smacked his lips thinking of these same things.

'I am, in short, no stoic,' he said, 'the stoics being ancient curmudgeons that were low-stomached.' Now, he continued, the Old Faith he loved well, but not over well; the Protestants he called busy knaves, but the New Learning he loved beyond life. Cromwell thwacked the Old Faith; he loved him not for that. Cromwell upheld in a sort the Protestants; he little loved him for that. 'But the New Learning he loveth, and, oh fair sharer of my dreams o' nights, Cromwell holdeth the strings of the money-bags.'

She scratched her cheek meditatively, and then unfolded her arms.

'How then ha' ye come by his broad pieces?'

'It is three years since,' he answered, 'that Privy Seal sent for me. I had been cast out of my mastership at Eton College, for they said—foul liars said—that I had stolen the silver salt-cellars.' He had been teaching, for his sins, in the house of the Lord Edmund Howard, where he had had his best pupil, but no more salary than what his belly could hold of poor mutton. 'So Privy Seal did send for me——'

'Kat Howard was thy best pupil?' his wife asked meditatively.

'By the shrine of Saint Eloi—' he commenced to swear.

'Nay, lie not,' she cut him short. 'You love Kat Howard and six other wenches. I know it well. What said Privy Seal?'

He meditated again to protest that he loved not Katharine, but her quiet stolidity set him to change his mind.

'It was that the Lady Mary of England needed a preceptor, an amanuensis, an aid for her studies in the learned language.' For the King's Highness' daughter had a great learning and was agate of writing a commentary of Plautus his plays. But the Lady Mary hated also virulently—and with what cause all men know—the King her father. And for years long, since the death of the Queen her mother—whom God preserve in Paradise!—for years long the Lady Mary had maintained a treasonable correspondence with the King's enemies, with the Emperor, with the Bishop of Rome——

'Our Holy Father the Pope,' his wife said, and crossed herself.

'And with this King here of France,' Udal continued, whilst he too crossed himself with graceful waves of his brown hand. He continued to report that the way in which the Lady Mary sent her letters abroad had never been found; that Cromwell had appointed three tutors in succession to be aid to the Lady Mary in her studies. Each of these three she had broken and cast out from her doors, she being by far the more learned, so that, though Privy Seal in his might had seven thousand spies throughout the realm of

England, he had among them no man learned enough to take this place and to spy out the things that he would learn.

'Therefore Privy Seal did send for thee, who art accounted the most learned doctor in Christendom.' His wife's eyes glowed and her face became ruddy with pride in her husband's fame.

The magister waved his hand pleasantly.

'Therefore he did send for me.' Privy Seal had promised him seven hundred pounds, farms with sixty pounds by the year, or the headship of New College if the magister could discover how the Lady Mary wrote her letters abroad.

'So I have stayed three years with the Lady Mary,' Udal said. 'But before God,' he asseverated, 'though I have known these twenty-nine months that she sent away her letters in the crusts of pudding pies, never hath cur Crummock had word of it.'

'A fool he, to set thee to spy upon a petticoat,' she answered pleasantly.

'Woman,' he answered hotly, 'crowns I have made by making reports to Privy Seal. I have set his men to watch doors and windows where none came in or entered; I have reported treasons of men whose heads had already fallen by the axe; I have told him of words uttered by maids of honour whom he knew full well already miscalled him. Sometimes I have had a crown or two from him, sometimes more; but no good man hath been hurt by my spying.'

'Husband,' she uttered, with her face set expressionlessly, 'knew ye that the Frenchman's cook that made the pudding pies had been taken and cast into the Tower gaol?'

Udal's arms flew above his head; his eyes started from their sockets; his tongue came forth from his pale mouth to lick his dry lips, and his legs failed him so that he sat himself down, wavering from side to side in the window-seat.

'Then the commentary of Plautus shall never be written,' he wailed. He wrung his hands. 'Whom have they taken else?' he said. 'How knew ye these things when I nothing knew? What make of house is this where such things be known?'

'Husband,' she answered, 'this house is even an inn. Where many travellers pass through, many secrets are known. I know of this cook's fate since the fate of cooks is much spoken of in kitchens, and this was the cook of a Frenchman, and this is France.'

'Save us, oh pitiful saints!' the magister whispered. 'Who else is taken? What more do ye know? Many others have aided. I too. And there be friends I love.'

'Husband,' she answered, 'I know no more than this: three days ago the cook stood where now you stand——'

He clasped his hair so that his cap fell to the ground.

'Here!' he said. 'But he was in the Tower!'

'He was in the Tower, but stood here free,' she answered. Udal groaned.

'Then he hath blabbed. We are lost.'

She answered:

'That may be the truth. But I think it is not. For so the matter is that the cook told me.' He was taken and set in the Tower by the men of Privy Seal. Yet within ten hours came the men of the King; these took him aboard a cogger, the cogger took them to Calais, and at the gate of Calais town the King's men kicked him into the country of France, he having sworn on oath never more to tread on English soil.

Udal groaned.

'Aye! But what others were taken? What others shall be?'

She shook her head.

The report ran: a boy called Poins, a lady called Elliott, and a lady called Howard. Yet all three drank the free air before that day at nightfall.

Udal, huddled against the wall, took these blows of fate with a quiver for each. In the back of the kitchen the servers, come down from the meal of the Cleves envoy, made a great clatter with their dishes of pewter and alloy. The hostess, working with her comfortable sway of the hips, drove them gently through the door to let a silence fall; but gradually Udal's jaw closed, his eyes grew smaller, he started suddenly and the muscles of his knees regained their tension. The hostess, swishing her many petticoats beneath her, sat down again on the stool.

'*Insipiens et infacetus quin sum!* the magister mused. 'Fool that I am! Wherefore see I no clue?' He hung his head; frowned; then started anew with his hand on his side.

'Wherefore shall I not read pure joy in this?' he said, 'save that Austin waileth: "*Inter delicias semper aliquid saevi nos strangulat.*" I would be joyful—but that I fear.' Norfolk had come upon an embassy here; then assuredly Cromwell's power waned, or never had this foe of his been sent in this office of honour. The cook was cast in the Tower, but set free by the King's men; young Poins was cast too, but set free—the Lady Elliott—and the Lady Howard. What then? What then?

'Husband,' she said, 'have you naught forgotten?'

Udal, musing with his hand upon his chin, shook his head negligently.

'I keep more track of the King's leman than thou, then,' she said. 'What was it Longstaffe said of her?'

'Nay,' Udal answered, 'so turned my bowels were with jealousy that little I noted.'

'Why, you are a fine spy,' she said. And she repeated to him that Longstaffe had reported the King's commanding Katharine and Privy Seal to join hands and be friends. Udal shook his head gloomily.

'I would not have my best pupil friends with Cromwell,' he said.

'Oh, magister,' she retorted, with a first touch of scorn in her voice; 'have you, who have had so much truck with women, yet to learn that you may command a woman to be friends with a man, yet no power on earth shall make her love him. Nevertheless, well might Cromwell seek to win her love, and thence these pardons.'

Udal started forward upon his tiptoes.

'I must to London!' he cried. She smiled at him as at a child.

'You are come to be of my advice,' she said.

Udal gazed at her with a wondering patronage.

'Why, what a wench it is,' he said, and he crooked his arm around her ample waist. His face shone with pleasure. 'Angel!' he uttered; 'for Angelos is the Greek for messenger, and signifieth more especially one that bringeth good tidings.' Out of all this holus bolus of envoys, ambassadors, cooks and prisoners one thing appeared plain to view: that, for the first time, *a solis ortus cardine*, Cromwell had loosened his grip of some that he held. 'And if Crummock looseneth grip, Crummock's power in the land waneth.'

She looked up at him with a coy pleasure.

'Hatest Cromwell then full fell-ly?' she asked.

He put his hands upon her shoulders and solemnly regarded her.

'Woman,' he said; 'this man rideth England with seven thousand spies; these three years I have lived in terror of my life. I have had no bliss that fear hath not entered into—in very truth *inter delicias semper aliquid saevi nos strangulavit.*' His lugubrious tones grew higher with hatred; he raised one hand above his head and one gripped tight her fat shoulder. 'Terror hath bestridden our realm of England; no man dares to whisper his hate even to the rushes. Me! Me! Me!' he reached a pitch of high-voiced fury. 'Me! *Virum doctissimum!* Me, the first learned man in Britain, he did force to write a play in the vulgar tongue. Me, a master of Latin, to write in English! I had pardoned him my terror. I had pardoned him the heads of the good men he hath struck off. For that princes should inspire terror is just, and that the great ones of the earth should prey one upon the other is a thing all history giveth precedent for since the days when Sylla hunted to death Marius that sat amidst the ruins of Carthage. But that the learned should be put to shame! that good letters should be cast into the mire! History showeth no ensample of a man so vile since the Emperor Alexander removed his shadow from before the tub of Diogenes.'

'In truth,' she said, blenching a little before his fury, 'I was ever one that loved the rolling sound of your Greek and your Roman.'

'Give me my journey money,' he said, 'let me begone to England. For, if indeed the Lady Katharine hath the King's ear, much may I aid her with my counsels.'

She began to fumble in beneath her apron, and then, as if she suddenly remembered herself, she placed her finger upon her lips.

'Husband,' she said, 'I have for you a gift. How it shall value itself to you I little know, but I have before been much besought and offered high payment for that which now I offer thee. Come.'

The finger still upon her plump lips, she led him to a small door behind the chimney stack. They climbed up through cobwebs, ham, flitches of smoked beef, and darkness, and the reek of wood-smoke, until they came, high up, to a store-room in the slope of a mansard roof. Light filtered dimly between the tiles, and many bales and sacks lay upon the raftered floor like huge monsters in a huge, dim cave.

'Hearken! make no sound,' she whispered, and in the intense gloom they heard a sullen, stertorous, intermittent rumble.

'The envoy sleeps,' she said. She set her eye to a knot-hole in the planked wall. "A sleeps!' she whispered. 'My pigling made a great thirst in him. Much wine he drank. Set your eye to the knot-hole.'

With his face glued against the rough wood, the magister could see in the large room a great fair man, in a great blue chair behind a littered table. His head hung forward, shewed only a pink bald spot in the thin hair, and brilliant red ears. A slow rumble of snoring came for a long minute, then ceased for as long.

From behind Udal's back came a crash, and he started back to see the large woman, who had overturned a chest.

'That is to test how he sleeps,' she said. 'See if he have moved.' The man, plain to see through the knot-hole, had stirred no muscle; again the heavy rumble of the snore came to them. She spoke quite loudly now. 'Why, naught shall wake him these five hours. 'A hath bolted the door; thus his secretaries shall not come to him. See now.'

She slid back a board in the wall, and Udal could see into what appeared to be a cupboard filled with a litter of papers and of parchments. Udal's heart began to beat so that he noted it there; his eyes searched hers with a glittering excitement—nevertheless a half fear of awakening the envoy kept him from speaking.

'Take them! Take them!' she nudged him with her elbow. 'Six hours ye have to read and to copy.'

'What papers are these?' he muttered, his voice thick betwixt incredulous joy and fear.

'They be the envoy's papers,' she said; 'doubtless these be his letters to the king of this land.... What there may be I know not else.'

Udal's hands were in at the hole with the swift clutch of a miser visiting his treasure-chest. The woman surveyed him with pleasure and with pride in her achievement, and with the calmness of routine she fitted a bar across the door of the cupboard where it opened into the envoy's room. Udal was fumbling already with the strings of a packet, his eyes searching the superscription in the gloom.

'Six hours ye have to read and to copy,' she said happily, 'for, for six hours the poppy seed in his wine that he drank shall surely keep him snoring.' And, whilst they went again down the stairway, the papers secreted beneath the magister's gown, she explained with her pride and happiness. The aumbry was so contrived that any envoy or secretary sleeping in her best room must needs put his papers therein, since there was in the room no other chest that locked. And the King of France's chancellors allotted to all envoys her hostelry for a lodging; and once there, she made them heavy with wine and poppy seed after a receipt she had from an Egyptian, and at the appointed time the King of France's men came to read through the papers and to pay her much money and many kisses.

It was six hours later that the magister stood in his own room crushing a fillet of papers into the breast of his brown jerkin. The hostess, walking always calmly as if disorder of the mind were a thing she were a stranger to, had reclimbed the narrow stairway, replaced the papers in the envoy's cupboard and returned to her husband. She sought, mutely, for commendations, and he gave her them.

'Y'have made me the man that holds the secret of England's future,' he said. 'All England that groans beneath Cromwell awaiteth to hear how the cat jumps in Cleves. Now I know how the cat jumps in Cleves.'

She wiped the dust from her hands upon her apron.

'See that ye make good use of the knowledge,' she said. She considered for a moment whilst he ferreted amongst his clothes in the great black press beside the great white bed. 'I have long thought,' she said, 'that greatly might I be of service to a man of laws and of policies. But I have long known that to serve a man is to have little reward unless a woman tie him up in fast bonds———' He made one of his broad gestures of negation, but she cut in upon his words: 'Aye, so it is. A gossip may serve a man how she will, but once his occasion is past he shall leave her in the ditch for the first fairer face. So I made resolve to make such a man my husband, that his being advanced might advance me. For, for sure this shall not be the last spying service I shall do thee. Many envoys more shall be lodged in this house and many more secrets ye shall learn.'

'Oh beloved Pandora!' he cried; 'opener of all secret places, caskets, aumbries, caves of the winds, thrice blessed Sibyl of the keyhole!' She nodded her head with grave contentment.

'I chose thee for thy resounding speeches,' she said. Her tranquillity and her buxom pleasantness overcame him with sudden affection. He was minded to tell her— because indeed she had made his fortunes for him—that her marriage to him did not hold good since a friar had read the rites.

'I chose thee for thy resounding speeches,' she said, 'and because art so ill-clothed i' the ribs. Give me a thin man of policies to move my bowels of compassion, say I.' For with her secret closets she might make him stand well among the princes, and with her goodly capons set grease upon his ribs, poor soul!

'Oh Guenevere!' he said; 'for was it not the queen of Arthur that made bag-puddings for his starving knights?'

'Aye,' she said; 'great learning you possess.' A little moisture bedewed her blue eyes. 'It grieves me that you must begone. I love to hear thy broad o's and a's!'

'Then by all that is fattest in the land hight Cokaigne I will stay here, thy dutiful goodman,' he said, and tears filled his own eyes.

'Oh nay,' she answered; 'you shall get yourself into the Chancellery, and merry will we feast and devise beneath the gilded roofs.' Her eyes sought the brown beams that ceiled the long room. 'I have heard that chancellors have always gilded roofs.'

Again the tenderness overcame him for the touch of simple pride in her voice. And the confession slipped from his lips:

'Poor befooled soul! Shalt never be a chancellor's dame.'

She was sobbing a little.

'Oh aye,' she said; 'thou shalt yet be chancellor, and I will baste thy cooks' ribs an they baste not thy meat full well.' Such a man as he would find favour with princes for his glosing tongue—aye, and with queens too. At that she covered her face with her apron, and from beneath it her voice came forth:

'If this Kat Howard come to be queen, shall not the old faith be restored?'

The recollection of this particular certainty affected the magister like a stab, for, if the old faith came back, then assuredly marriages by friars should again be acknowledged. He cursed himself beneath his breath: he was loath to leave the woman in the ditch, her trusting face and pleasing ways stirred the strings of his heart. But he was more than loath that the wedding should hold a wedding. He shook his perplexity from him with starting towards the door.

'Time to be gone!' he said, and added, 'Be certain and take care that no Englishman heareth of wedding betwixt thee and me.' It must in England work his sure undoing.

She removed her apron and nodded gravely.

'Aye,' she said, 'that is certain enow with Court ladies, such as they be to-day.' But she asked that when he went among women she should hear nothing of it. For she had had three husbands and several courtiers to prove it upon, that it is better to be lied to than to know truth.

'There is in the world no woman like to thee!' he said with a great sincerity. Once more she nodded.

'Aye, that is the lie that I would hear,' she said. On his part, he started suddenly with pain.

'But thee!' he uttered.

'Aye,' she cried again, 'that too is needed. But be very certain of this, that not easily will I plant upon thy brow that which most husbands wear!' She paused, and once more rubbed her hands. Courteous she must be, since her calling called therefor. But assuredly, having had three husbands, she had had embraces enow to crave little for men. And, if she did that which few good women have a need to—save very piteous women in ballads—she would suffer him to belabour her;—she nodded again—'And that to a man is a great solace.'

He fled with precipitancy from the thought of this solace, brushing through the narrow passages, stalking across the great guest-chamber and the greater kitchen where, in the falling dusk, the fires glowed red upon the maids' faces and the cooks' aprons, the smoke rose unctuously upward tended with rich smells of meat, and the windjacks clanked in the chimneys. She trotted behind him, weeping in the gloaming.

'If you come to be chancellor in five years,' she whimpered, 'I shall come across the seas to ye. If ye fail, this shall be your plenteous house.'

Whilst she hung round his neck in the shadowy courtyard and he had already one foot in the stirrup, she begged for one more great speech.

'Before Jupiter!' he said, 'I can think of none for crying!'

The big black horse, with its bags before and behind the saddle, stirred, so that, standing upon one foot, he fell away from her. But he swung astride the saddle, his cloak flying, his long legs clasping round the belly. It reared and pawed the twilight mists, but he smote it over one ear with his palm, and it stood trembling.

'This is a fine beast y'have given me,' he said, pleasure thrilling his limbs.

'I have given it a fine rider!' she cried. He wheeled it near her and stooped right down to kiss her face. He was very sure in his saddle, having learned the trick of the stirrup from old Rowfant, that had taught the King.

'Wife,' he said, 'I have bethought me of this: *Post equitem sedet*——' He faltered—'*sedet—Behind the rider sitteth*—But for the life of me I know not whether it be *atra cura* or no.'

And, as he left Paris gates behind him and speeded towards the black hills, bending low to face the cold wind of night, for the life of him he knew not whether black care sat behind him or no. Only, as night came down and he sped forward, he knew that he was speeding for England with the great news that the Duke of Cleves was seeking to make his peace with the Emperor and the Pope through the mediancy of the king of that land and, on the soft road, the hoofs of the horse seemed to beat out the rhythm of the words:

'Crummock is down: Cromwell is down. Crummock is down: Cromwell is down.'

He rode all through the night thinking of these things, for, because he carried letters from the English ambassador to the King of England, the gates of no small town could stay his passing through.

IV

Five men talked in the long gallery overlooking the River Thames. It was in the Lord Cromwell's house, upon which the April showers fell like handsful of peas, with a sifting sound, between showers of sunshine that fell themselves like rain, so that at times all the long empty gallery was gilded with light and at times it was all saddened and frosty. They were talking all, and all with earnestness and concern, as all the Court and the city were talking now, of Katharine Howard whom the King loved.

The Archbishop leant against one side of a window, close beside him his spy Lascelles; the Archbishop's face was round but worn, his large eyes bore the trace of sleeplessness, his plump hands were a little tremulous within his lawn sleeves.

'Sir,' he said, 'we must bow to the breeze. In time to come we may stand straight enow.' His eyes seemed to plead with Privy Seal, who paced the gallery in short, pursy strides, his plump hands hidden in the furs behind his back. Lascelles, the Archbishop's spy, nodded his head sagaciously; his yellow hair came from high on his crown and was brushed forward towards his brows. He did not speak, being in such high company, but looking at him, the Archbishop gained confidence from the support of his nod.

'If we needs must go with the Lady Katharine towards Rome,' he pleaded again, 'consider that it is but for a short time.' Cromwell passed him in his pacing and, unsure of having caught his ear, Cranmer addressed himself to Throckmorton and Wriothesley, the two men of forty who stood gravely, side by side, fingering their long beards. 'For sure,' Cranmer appealed to the three silent men, 'what we must avoid is crossing the King's Highness. For his Highness, crossed, hath a swift and sudden habit of action.' Wriothesley nodded, and: 'Very sudden,' Lascelles allowed himself utterance, in a low voice. Throckmorton's eyes alone danced and span; he neither nodded nor spoke, and, because he was thought to have a great say in the councils of Privy Seal, it was to him that Cranmer once more addressed himself urgently:

'Full-bodied men who are come upon failing years are very prone to women. 'Tis a condition of the body, a humour, a malady that passeth. But, while it lasteth, it must be bowed to.'

Cromwell, with his deaf face, passed once more before them. He addressed himself in brief, sharp tones to Wriothesley:

'You say, in Paris an envoy from Cleves was come a week agone?' and passed on.

'It must be bowed to,' Cranmer continued his speech. 'I do maintain it. There is no way but to divorce the Queen.' Again Lascelles nodded; it was Wriothesley this time who spoke.

'It is a lamentable thing!' and there was a heavy sincerity in his utterance, his pose, with his foot weightily upon the ground, being that of an honest man. 'But I do think you have the right of it. We, and the new faith with us, are between Scylla and Charybdis. For certain, our two paths do lie between divorcing the Queen and seeing you, great lords, who so well defend us, cast down.'

Coming up behind him, Cromwell placed a hand upon his shoulder.

'Goodly knight,' he said, 'let us hear thy thoughts. His Grace's of Canterbury we do know very well. He is for keeping a whole skin!'

Cranmer threw up his hands, and Lascelles looked at the ground. Throckmorton's eyes were filled with admiration of this master of his that he was betraying now. He muttered in his long, golden beard.

'Pity we must have thy head.'

Wriothesley cleared his throat, and having considered, spoke earnestly.

'It is before all things expedient and necessary,' he said, 'that we do keep you, my Lord Privy Seal, and you, my Lord of Canterbury, at the head of the State.' That was above all necessary. For assuredly this land, though these two had brought it to a great pitch of wealth, clean living, true faith and prosperity, this land needed my Lord Privy Seal before all men to shield it from the treason of the old faith. There were many lands now, bringing wealth and commodity to the republic, that should soon again revert towards and pay all their fruits to Rome; there were many cleaned and whitened churches that should again hear the old nasty songs and again be tricked with gewgaws of the idolaters. Therefore, before all things, my Lord Privy Seal must retain the love of the King's Highness—— Cromwell, who had resumed his pacing, stayed for a moment to listen.

'Wherefore brought ye not news of why Cleves' envoy came to Paris town?' he said pleasantly. 'All the door turneth upon that hinge.'

Wriothesley stuttered and reddened.

'What gold could purchase, I purchased of news,' he said. 'But this envoy would not speak; his knaves took my gold and had no news. The King of France's men——'

'Oh aye,' Cromwell continued; 'speak on about the other matter.'

Wriothesley turned his slow mind from his vexation in Paris, whence he had come a special journey to report of the envoy from Cleves. He spoke again swiftly, turning right round to Cromwell.

'Sir,' he said, 'study above all to please the King. For unless you guide us we are lost indeed.'

Cromwell worked his lips one upon another and moved a hand.

'Aye,' Wriothesley continued; 'it can be done only by bringing the King's Highness and the Lady Katharine to a marriage.'

'Only by that?' Cromwell asked enigmatically.

Throckmorton spoke at last:

'Your lordship jests,' he said; 'since the King is not a man, but a high and beneficent prince with a noble stomach.'

Cromwell tapped him upon the cheek.

'That you do see through a millstone I know,' he said. 'But I was minded to hear how these men do think. You and I do think alike.'

'Aye, my lord,' Throckmorton answered boldly. 'But in ten minutes I must be with the Lady Katharine, and I am minded to hear the upshot of this conference.'

Cromwell laughed at him sunnily:

'Go and do your message with the lady. An you hasten, you may return ere ever this conference ends, since slow wits like ours need a store of words to speak their minds with.'

Lascelles, the silent spy of the archbishop, devoured with envious eyes Throckmorton's great back and golden beard. For his life he dared not speak three words unbidden in this company. But Throckmorton being gone the discussion renewed itself, Wriothesley speaking again.

He voiced always the same ideas, for the same motives: Cromwell must maintain his place at the cost of all things, for the sake of all these men who leaned upon him. And it was certain that the King loved this lady. If he had sent her few gifts and given her no titles nor farms, it was because—either of nature or to enhance the King's appetite—she shewed a prudish disposition. But day by day and week in week out the King went with his little son in his times of ease to the rooms of the Lady Mary. And there he went, assuredly, not to see the glum face of the daughter that hated him, but to converse in Latin with his daughter's waiting-maid of honour. All the

Court knew this. Who there had not seen how the King smiled when he came new from the Lady Mary's rooms? He was heavy enow at all other times. This fair woman that hated alike the new faith and all its ways had utterly bewitched and enslaved the King's eyes, ears and understanding. If the King would have Katharine Howard his wife the King must have her. Anne of Cleves must be sent back to Germany; Cromwell must sue for peace with the Howard wench; a way must be found to bribe her till the King tired of her; then Katharine must go in her turn, once more Cromwell would have his own, and the Protestants be reinstated. Cromwell retained his silence; at the last he uttered his unfailing words with which he closed all these discussions:

'Well, it is a great matter.'

The gusts of rain and showers of sun pursued each other down the river; the lights and shadows succeeded upon the cloaked and capped shapes of the men who huddled their figures together in the tall window. At last the Archbishop lost his patience and cried out:

'What will you *do*? What will you *do*?'

Cromwell swung his figure round before him.

'I will discover what Cleves will do in this matter,' he said. 'All dependeth therefrom.'

'Nay; make a peace with Rome,' Cranmer uttered suddenly. 'I am weary of these strivings.'

But Wriothesley clenched his fist.

'Before ye shall do that I will die, and twenty thousand others!'

Cranmer quailed.

'Sir,' he temporised. 'We will give back to the Bishop of Rome nothing that we have taken of property. But the Bishop of Rome may have Peter's Pence and the deciding of doctrines.'

'Canterbury,' Wriothesley said, 'I had rather Antichrist had his old goods and gear in this realm than the handling of our faith.'

Cromwell drew in the air through his nostrils, and still smiled.

'Be sure the Bishop of Rome shall have no more gear and no more guidance of this realm than his Highness and I need give,' he said. 'No stranger shall have any say in the councils of this realm.' He smiled noiselessly again. 'Still and still, all turneth upon Cleves.'

For the first time Lascelles spoke:

'All turneth upon Cleves,' he said.

Cromwell surveyed him, narrowing his eyes.

'Speak you now of your wisdom,' he uttered with neither friendliness nor contempt. Lascelles caressed his shaven chin and spoke:

'The King's Highness I have observed to be a man for women—a man who will give all his goods and all his gear to a woman. Assuredly he will not take this woman to his leman; his princely stomach revolteth against an easy won mastership. He will pay dear, he will pay his crown to win her. Yet the King would not give his policies. Neither would he retrace his steps for a woman's sake unless Fate too cried out that he must.'

Cromwell nodded his head. It pleased him that this young man set a virtue sufficiently high upon his prince.

'Sirs,' he said, 'daily have I seen this King in ten years, and I do tell ye no man knoweth how the King loves kingcraft as I know.' He nodded again to Lascelles, whose small stature seemed to gain bulk, whose thin voice seemed to gain volume from this approval and from his 'Speak on. About Cleves.'

'Sirs,' Lascelles spoke again, 'whiles there remains the shade of a chance that Cleves' Duke shall lead the princes of Germany against the Emperor and France, assuredly the King shall stay his longing for the Lady Katharine. He shall stay firm in his marriage with the Queen.' Again Cromwell nodded. 'Till then it booteth little to move towards a divorce; but if that day should come, then our Lord Privy Seal must bethink himself. That is in our lord's mind.'

'By Bacchus!' Cromwell said, 'your Grace of Canterbury hath a jewel in your crony and helper. And again I say, we must wait upon Cleves.' He seemed to pursue the sunbeams along the gallery, then returned to say:

'I know ye know I love little to speak my mind. What I think or how I will act I keep to myself. But this I will tell you:' Cleves might have two minds in sending to France an envoy. On the one hand, he might be minded to abandon Henry and make submission to the Emperor and to Rome. For, in the end, was not the Duke of Cleves a vassal of the Emperor? It might be that. Or it might be that he was sending merely to ask the King of France to intercede betwixt him and his offended lord. The Emperor was preparing to wage war upon Cleves. That was known. And doubtless Cleves, desiring to retain his friendship with Henry, might have it in mind to keep friends with both. There the matter hinged, Cromwell repeated. For, if Cleves remained loyal to the King of England, Henry would hear nothing of divorcing Cleves' sister, and would master his desire for Katharine.

'Believe me when I speak,' Cromwell added earnestly. 'Ye do wrong to think of this King as a lecher after the common report. He is a man very continent for a king. His kingcraft cometh before all women. If the Duke of Cleves be firm friend to him, firm friend he will be to the Duke's sister. The Lady Howard will be his friend, but the Lady Howard will be neither his leman nor his guide to Rome. He will please her if he may. But his kingcraft. Never!' He broke off and laughed noiselessly at the Archbishop's face of dismay. 'Your Grace would make a pact with Rome?' he asked.

'Why, these are very evil times,' Cranmer answered. 'And if the Bishop of Rome will give way to us, why may we not give pence to the Bishop of Rome?'

'Goodman,' Cromwell answered, 'these are evil times because we men are evil.' He pulled a paper from his belt. 'Sirs,' he said, 'will ye know what manner of woman this Katharine Howard is?' and to their murmurs of assent: 'This lady hath asked to speak with me. Will ye hear her speak? Then bide ye here. Throckmorton is gone to seek her.'

V

Katharine Howard sat in her own room; it had in it little of sumptuousness, for all the King so much affected her. It was the room she had first had at Hampton after coming to be maid to the King's daughter, and it had the old, green hangings that had always been round the walls, the long oak table, the box-bed set in the wall, the high chair and the three stools round the fire. The only thing she had taken of the King was a curtain in red cloth to hang on a rod before the door where was a great draught, the leading of the windows being rotted. She had lived so poor a life, her father having been a very poor lord with many children—she was so attuned to flaws of the wind, ill-feeding and harsh clothes, that such a tall room as she there had seemed goodly enough for her. Barely three months ago she had come to the palace of Greenwich riding upon a mule. Now accident, or maybe the design of the dear saints, had set her so high in the King's esteem that she might well try a fall with Privy Seal.

She sat there dressed, awaiting the summons to go to him. She wore a long dress of red velvet, worked around the breast-lines with little silver anchors and hearts, and her hood was of black lawn and fell near to her hips behind. And she had read and learned by heart passages from Plutarch, from Tacitus, from Diodorus Siculus, from Seneca and from Tully, each one inculcating how salutary a thing in a man was the love of justice. Therefore she felt herself well prepared to try a fall with the chief enemy of her faith, and awaited with impatience his summons to speak with him. For she was anxious, now at last, to speak out her mind, and Privy Seal's agents had worked upon the religious of a poor little convent near her father's house a wrong so baleful that she could no longer contain herself. Either Privy Seal must redress or she must go to the King for justice to these poor women that had taught her the very elements of virtue and lay now in gaol.

So she spoke to her two chief friends, her that had been Cicely Elliott and her old husband Rochford, the knight of Bosworth Hedge. They happened in upon her just after she was attired and had sent her maid to fetch her dinner from the buttery.

'Three months agone,' she said, 'the King's Highness did bid me cease from crying out upon Privy Seal; and not the King's Highness' self can say that in that time I have spoken word against the Lord Cromwell.'

Cicely Elliott, who dressed, in spite of her new wedding, all in black for the sake of some dead men, laughed round at her from her little stool by the fire.

'God help you! that must have been hard, to keep thy tongue from the flail of all Papists.'

The old knight, who was habited like Katharine, all in red, because at that season the King favoured that colour, pulled nervously at his little goat's beard, for all conversations that savoured of politics and religion were to him very fearful. He stood back against the green hangings and fidgeted with his feet.

But Katharine, who for the love of the King had been silent, was now set to speak her mind.

'It is Seneca,' she said, 'who tells us to have a check upon our tongues, but only till the moment approaches to speak.'

'Aye, goodman Seneca!' Cicely laughed round at her. Katharine smoothed her hair, but her eyes gleamed deeply.

'The moment approaches,' she said; 'I do like my King, but better I like my Church.' She swallowed in her throat. 'I had thought,' she said, 'that Privy Seal would stay his harryings of the goodly nuns in this land.' But now she had a petition, come that day from Lincoln gaol. Cromwell's servants were more bitter still than ever against the religious. Here was a false accusation of treason against her foster-mother's self. 'I will soon end it or mend it, or lose mine own head,' Katharine ended.

'Aye, pull down Cur Crummock,' Cicely said. 'I think the King shall not long stay away from thy desires.'

The old knight burst in:

'I take it ill that ye speak of these things. I take it ill. I will not have 'ee lose thy head in these quarrels.'

'Husband,' Cicely laughed round at him, 'three years ago Cur Crummock had the heads of all my menfolk, having sworn they were traitors.'

'The more reason that he have not mine and thine now,' the old knight answered grimly. 'I am not for these meddlings in things that concern neither me nor thee.'

Cicely Elliott set her elbows upon her knees and her chin upon her knuckles. She gazed into the fire and grew moody, as was her wont when she had chanced to think of her menfolk that Cromwell had executed.

'He might have had my head any day this four years,' she said. 'And had you lost my head and me you might have had any other maid any day that se'nnight.'

'Nay, I grow too old,' the knight answered. 'A week ago I dropped my lance.'

Cicely continued to gaze at nothings in the fire.

'For thee,' she said scornfully to Katharine, 'it were better thou hadst never been born than have meddled between kings and ministers and faiths and nuns. You are not made for this world. You talk too much. Get you across the seas to a nunnery.'

Katharine looked at her pitifully.

'Child,' she said, 'it was not I that spoke of thy menfolk.'

'Get thyself mewed up,' Cicely repeated more hotly; 'thou wilt set all this world by the ears. This is no place for virtues learned from learned books. This is an ill world where only evil men flourish.'

The old knight still fidgeted to be gone.

'Nay,' Katharine said seriously, 'ye think I will work mine own advantage with the King. But I do swear to thee I have it not in my mind.'

'Oh, swear not,' Cicely mumbled, 'all the world knoweth thee to be that make of fool.'

'I would well to get me made a nun—but first I will bring nunneries back from across the seas to this dear land.'

Cicely laughed again—for a long and strident while.

'You will come to no nunnery if you wait till then,' she said. 'Nuns without their heads have no vocation.'

'When Cromwell is down, no woman again shall lose her head,' Katharine answered hotly.

Cicely only laughed.

'No woman again!' Katharine repeated.

'Blood was tasted when first a queen fell on Tower Hill.' Cicely pointed her little finger at her. 'And the taste of blood, even as the taste of wine, ensureth a certain oblivion.'

'You miscall your King,' Katharine said.

Cicely laughed and answered: 'I speak of my world.'

Katharine's blood came hot to her cheeks.

'It is a new world from now on,' she answered proudly.

'Till a new queen's blood seal it an old one,' Cicely mocked her earnestness. 'Hadst best get thee to a nunnery across the seas.'

'The King did bid me bide here.' Katharine faltered in the least.

'You have spoken of it with him?' Cicely said. 'Why, God help you!'

Katharine sat quietly, her fair hair gilded by the pale light of the gusty day, her lips parted a little, her eyelids drooping. It behoved her to move little, for her scarlet dress was very nice in its equipoise, and fain she was to seem fine in Privy Seal's eyes.

'This King hath a wife to his tail,' Cicely mocked her.

The old knight had recovered his quiet; he had his hand upon his haunch, and spoke with his air of wisdom:

'I would have you to cease these talkings of dangerous things,' he said. 'I am Rochford of Bosworth Hedge. I have kept my head and my lands, and my legs from chains—and how but by leaving to talk of dangerous things?'

Katharine moved suddenly in her chair. This speech, though she had heard it a hundred times before, struck her now as so craven that she forgot alike her desire to keep fine and her friendship for the old man's new wife.

'Aye, you have been a coward all your life,' she said: for were not her dear nuns in Lincoln gaol, and this was a knight that should have redressed wrongs!

Old Rochford smiled with his air of tranquil wisdom and corpulent age.

'I have struck good blows,' he said. 'There have been thirteen ballads writ of me.'

'You have kept so close a tongue,' Katharine said to him hotly, 'that I know not what you love. Be you for the old faith, or for this Church of devils that Cromwell hath set up in the land? Did you love Queen Katharine or Queen Anne Boleyn? Were you glad when More died, or did you weep? Are you for the Statute of Users, or would you end it? Are you for having the Lady Mary called bastard—God pardon me the word!—or would you defend her with your life?—I do not know. I have spoken with you many times—but I do not know.'

Old Rochford smiled contentedly.

'I have saved my head and my lands in these perilous times by letting no man know,' he said.

'Aye,' Katharine met his words with scorn and appeal. 'You have kept your head on your shoulders and the rent from your lands in your poke. But oh, sir, it is certain that, being a man, you love either the new ways or the old; it is certain that, being a spurred knight, you should love the old ways. Sir, bethink you and take heed of this: that the angels of God weep above England, that the Mother of God weeps above England; that the saints of God do weep—and you, a spurred knight, do wield a good sword. Sir, when you stand before the gates of Heaven, what shall you answer the warders thereof?'

'Please God,' the old knight answered, 'that I have struck some good blows.'

'Aye; you have struck blows against the Scots,' Katharine said. 'But the beasts of the field strike as well against the foes of their kind—the bull of the herd against lions; the Hyrcanian tiger against the troglodytes; the basilisk against many beasts. It is the province of a man to smite not only against the foes of his kind but—and how much the more?—against the foes of his God.'

In the full flow of her speaking there came in the great, blonde Margot Poins, her body-maid. She led by the hand the Magister Udal, and behind them followed, with his foxy eyes and long, smooth beard, the spy Throckmorton, vivid in his coat of green and scarlet stockings. And, at the antipathy of his approach, Katharine's emotions grew the more harrowing—as if she were determined to shew this evil supporter of her cause how a pure fight should be waged. They moved on tiptoe and stood against the hangings at the back.

She stretched out her hands to the old knight.

'Here you be in a pitiful and afflicted land from which the saints have been driven out; have you struck one blow for the saints of God? Nay, you have held your peace. Here you be where good men have been sent to the block: have you decried their fates? You have seen noble and beloved women, holy priests, blessed nuns defiled and martyred; you have seen the poor despoiled; you have seen that knaves ruled by aid of the devil about a goodly king. Have you struck one blow? Have you whispered one word?'

The colour rushed into Margot Poins' huge cheeks. She kept her mouth open to drink in her mistress's words, and Throckmorton waved his hands in applause. Only Udal shuffled in his broken-toed shoes, and old Rochford smiled benignly and tapped his chest above the chains.

'I have struck good blows in the quarrels that were mine,' he answered.

Katharine wrung her hands.

'Sir, I have read it in books of chivalry, the province of a knight is to succour the Church of God, to defend the body of God, to set his lance in rest for the Mother of God; to defend noble men cast down, and noble women; to aid holy priests and blessed nuns; to succour the despoiled poor.'

'Nay, I have read no books of chivalry,' the old man answered; 'I cannot read.'

'Ah, there be pitiful things in this world,' Katharine said, and her chest was troubled.

'You should quote Hesiodus,' Cicely mocked her suddenly from her stool. 'I marked this text when all my menfolk were slain: πλείη μὲν γὰρ γᾶια, πλείη δὲ θάλασσα so I have laughed ever since.'

Upon her, too, Katharine turned.

'You also,' she said; 'you also.'

'No, before God, I am no coward,' Cicely Elliott said. 'When all my menfolk were slain by the headsman something broke in my head, and ever since I have laughed. But before God, in my way I have tried to plague Cromwell. If he would have had my head he might have.'

'Yet what hast thou done for the Church of God?' Katharine said.

Cicely Elliott sprang to the floor and raised her hands with such violence that Throckmorton moved swiftly forward.

'What did the Church of God for me?' she cried. 'Guard your face from my nails ere you ask me that again. I had a father; I had two brothers; I had two men I loved passing well. They all died upon one day upon the one block. Did the saints of God save them? Go see their heads upon the gates of York?'

'But if they died for God His pitiful sake,' Katharine said—'if they did die in the quarrel of God's wounds——'

Cicely Elliott screamed, with her hands above her head.

'Is that not enow? Is that not enow?'

'Then it is I, not thou, that love them,' Katharine said; 'for I, not thou, shall carry on the work for which they died.'

'Oh gaping, pink-faced fool!' Cicely Elliott sneered at her.

She began to laugh, holding her black sides in, her face thrown back. Then she closed her mouth and stood smiling.

'You were made for a preacher, coney,' she said. 'Fine to hear thee belabouring my old, good knight with doughty words.'

'Gibe as thou wilt; scream as thou wilt——' Katharine began. Cicely Elliott tossed in on her words:

'My head ached so. I had the right of it to scream. I cannot be minded of my menfolk but my head will ache. But I love thy fine preaching. Preach on.'

Katharine raised herself from her chair.

'Words there must be that will move thee,' she said, 'if God will give them to me.'

'God hath withdrawn Himself from this world,' Cicely answered. 'All mankind goeth a-mumming.'

'It was another thing that Polycrates said.' Katharine, in spite of her emotion, was quick to catch the misquotation.

'Coney,' Cicely Elliott answered, 'all men wear masks; all men lie; all men desire the goods of all men and seek how they may get them.'

'But Cromwell being down, these things shall change,' Katharine answered. '*Res, aetas, usus, semper aliquid apportent novi.*'

Cicely Elliott fell back into her chair and laughed.

'What are we amongst that multitude?' she said. 'Listen to me: When my menfolk were cast to die, I flew to Gardiner to save them. Gardiner would not speak. Now is he Bishop of Winchester—for he had goods of my father's, and greased with them the way to his bishop's throne. Fanshawe is a goodly Papist; but Cromwell hath let him have goods of the Abbey of Bright. Will Fanshawe help thee to bring back the Church? Then he must give up his lands. Will Cranmer help thee? Will Miners? Coney, I loved Federan, a true man: Miners hath his land to-day, and Federan's mother starves. Will Miners help thee to gar the King do right? Then the mother of my love Federan must have Miners' land and the rents for seven years. Will Cranmer serve thee to bring back the Bishop of Rome? Why, Cranmer would burn.'

'But the poorer sort——' Katharine said.

'There is no man will help thee whose help will avail,' Cicely mocked at her. 'For hear me: No man now is up in the land that hath not goods of the Church; fields of the abbeys; spoons made of the parcel gilt from the shrines. There is no rich man now but is rich with stolen riches; there is no man now up that was not so set up. And the men that be down have lost their heads. Go dig in graves to find men that shall help thee.'

'Cromwell shall fall ere May goeth out,' Katharine said.

'Well, the King dotes upon thy sweet face. But Cromwell being down, there will remain the men he hath set up. Be they lovers of the old faith, or thee? Now, thy pranks will ruin all alike.'

'The King is minded to right these wrongs,' Katharine protested hotly.

'The King! The King!' Cicely laughed. 'Thou lovest the King.... Nay an thou lovest the King.... But to be enamoured of the King.... And the King enamoured of thee ... why, this pair of lovers cast adrift upon the land——'

Katharine said:

'Belike I am enamoured of the King: belike the King of me, I do not know. But this I know: he and I are minded to right the wrongs of God.'

Cicely Elliott opened her eyes wide.

'Why, thou art a very infectious fanatic!' she said. 'You may well do these things. But you must shed much blood. You must widow many men's wives. Body of God! I believe thou wouldst.'

'God forbid it!' Katharine said. 'But if He so willeth it, *fiat voluntas*.'

'Why, spare no man,' Cicely answered. 'Thou shalt not very easily escape.'

It was at this point that the magister was moved to keep no longer silence.

'Now, by all the gods of high Olympus!' he cried out, 'such things shall not be alleged against me. For I do swear, before Venus and all the saints, that I am your man.'

Nevertheless, it was Margot Poins, wavering between her love for her magister and her love for her mistress, that most truly was carried away by Katharine's eloquence.

'Mistress,' she said, and she indicated both the magister and his tall and bearded companion, 'these two have made up a pretty plot upon the stairs. There are in it papers from Cleves and a matter of deceiving Privy Seal and thou shouldst be kept in ignorance asking to—to——'

Her gruff voice failed and her blushes overcame her, so that she wanted for a word. But upon the mention of papers and Privy Seal the old knight fidgeted and faltered:

'Why, let us begone.' Cicely Elliott glanced from one to the other of them with a malicious glee, and Throckmorton's eyes blinked sardonically above his beard.

It had been actually upon the stairs that he had come upon the magister, newly down from his horse, and both stiff and bruised, with Margot Poins hanging about his neck and begging him to spare her a moment. Throckmorton crept up the dark stairway with his shoes soled with velvet. The magister was seeking to disengage himself from the girl with the words that he had a treaty form of the Duke of Cleves in his bosom and must hasten on the minute to give it to her mistress.

'Before God!' Throckmorton had said behind his back, 'ye will do no such thing,' and Udal had shrieked out like a rabbit caught by a ferret in its bury. For here he had seemed to find himself caught by the chief spy of Privy Seal upon a direct treason against Privy Seal's self.

But, dragging alike the terrified magister and the heavy, blonde girl who clung to him out from the dark stairhead into the corridor, where, since no one could come upon them unseen or unheard, it was the safest place in the palace to speak, Throckmorton had whispered into his ear a long, swift speech in which he minced no matters at all.

The time, he said, was ripe to bring down Privy Seal. He himself— Throckmorton himself—loved Kat Howard with a love compared to which the magister's was a rushlight such as you bought fifty for a halfpenny. Privy Seal was ravening for a report of that treaty. They must, before all things, bring him a report that was false. For, for sure, upon that report Privy Seal would act, and, if they brought him a false report, Privy Seal would act falsely.

Udal stood perfectly still, looking at nothing, his thin brown hand clasped round his thin brown chin.

'But, above all,' Throckmorton had concluded, 'show ye no papers to Kat Howard. For it is very certain that she will have no falsehoods employed to bring down Privy Seal, though she hate him as the Assyrian cockatrice hateth the symbol of the Cross.'

'Sir Throckmorton,' Margot Poins had uttered, 'though ye be a paid spy, ye speak true words there.'

He pulled his beard and blinked at her.

'I am minded to reform,' he said. 'Your mistress hath worked a miracle of conversion in me.'

She shrugged her great fair shoulders at this, and spoke to the magister:

'It is very true,' she said, 'that this spying knight affects my mistress. But whether it be for the love of virtue, or for the love of her body, or because the cat jumps that way and there he observeth fortune to rise, I leave to God who reads all hearts.'

'There speaks a wench brought up and taught by Protestants,' Throckmorton gibed pleasantly at her; 'or ye have caught the trick of Kat Howard, who, though she be a Papist as good as I, yet prates virtue like a Lutheran.'

'Ye lie!' Margot said; 'my mistress getteth her virtue from good letters.'

Throckmorton smiled at her again.

'Wench,' he said, 'in all save doctrine, this Kat Howard and her learning are nearer Lutheran than of the old faith.'

With his malice he set himself to bewilder Margot. They made a little, shadowy knot in the long corridor. For he wished to give Udal, who in his long gown stood deaf-faced, like a statue of contemplation, the time to come to a conclusion.

'Why, you are a very mean wag,' Margot said. 'I have heard my uncle—who is, as ye wot, a Protestant and a printer—I have heard him speak of Luther and of Bucer and of the word of God and suchlike canting books, but never once of Seneca and Tully, that my mistress loves.'

'Why, ye are learning the trick of tongues,' Throckmorton mocked. 'Please God, when your mistress cometh to be Queen—may He send it soon!— there shall be such a fashion and contagion of talking——'

Having his eyes on Udal, he broke off suddenly, and said with a harsh sharpness:

'I have given you time to make a resolution. Speak quickly. Will you come into our boat with us that will bring down Privy Seal?'

Udal winced, but Throckmorton held him by the wrist.

'Then unpouch quickly thy Cleves papers,' he said; 'we have but a little time to turn them round.'

Udal's thin hand sought nervously the opening of his jerkin beneath his gown: he drew it back, moved it forward again, and stood quivering with doubt.

Throckmorton stood vaingloriously back upon his feet and combed his great beard with his white fingers.

'Magister,' he uttered triumphantly, 'well you wot that such a man as you cannot plot for himself alone; you will make naught of your treasure trove save a cleft neck!'

And, furtively, cringing back into the dark hangings, a bent, broken figure like a miser unpouching his gold, Udal undid his breast lacings.

It was hot from this colloquy that Margot Poins had led the two men in upon her mistress in her large dim room. Because she hated the great spy, since he loved Kat Howard and had undone many good men with false tales, she had not been able to keep her tongue from seeking to wound him.

'Ye are too true to mix in plots,' she brought out gruffly.

Cicely Rochford came close to Katharine and measured her neck with the span of her small hand.

'There is room!' she said. 'Hast a long and a straight neck.'

Her husband muttered that he liked not these talkings. By diligent avoidance of such, he had kept his own hair and neck uncut in troublesome times.

'I will take thee to another place,' Cicely threw at him over her shoulder. 'Shalt kiss me in a dark room. It is very certain maids' talk is no fit hearing for thy jolly old ears.'

She took him delicately at the end of his short white beard between her long finger and thumb, and, with her high and mincing step, led him through the door.

'God save this room, where all the virtues bide!' she cried out, and drew her overskirt closer to her as she passed near the great, bearded spy.

Katharine turned and faced Throckmorton.

It is even as the maid saith,' she uttered. 'I am too true to mix in plots.'

'Neither will ye give us to death!' Throckmorton faced her back so that she paused for breath, and the pause lasted a full minute.

'Sir,' she said, 'I do give you a fair and a full warning that, if you do plot against Privy Seal, and if knowledge of your plotting cometh to mine ears—though I ask not to know of them—I will tell of your plottings——'

'Oh, before God!' Udal cried out, 'I have suckled you with learned writers; I have carried letters for you; will you give me to die?' and Margot wailed from a deep chest: 'The magister so well hath loved thee. Give him not into die hands of Cur Crummock!—would I had never told thee that they plotted!'

'Fool!' Throckmorton said; 'it is to the King she will go with her tales.' He sat down upon her yellow-wood table and swung one crimson leg before the other, laughing gleefully at Katharine's astonished face.

'Sir,' she said at last; 'it is true that I will go, not to my lord Privy Seal, but to the King.'

Throckmorton held up one of his white hands to the light and, with the other, smoothed down its little finger.

'See you?' he gibed softly at Margot. 'How better I guess this thing, mistress, than thou. For I do know her better.'

Katharine looked at him with a soft glance and said pitifully:

'Nevertheless, what shall it profit thee if I take a tale of thy treasons to the King's Highness?'

Throckmorton sprang from the table and clapped his heels together on the floor.

'It shall get me made an earl,' he said. 'The King will do that much for the man that shall rid him of his minister.' He reflected foxily and for a quick moment. 'Before God!' he said,'take this tale to the King, for it is the true tale: That the Duke of Cleves seeks, in France, to have done with his alliance. He will no more cleave to his brother-in-law, but will make submission to the Emperor and to Rome!'

He paused, and then finished:

'For that news the King shall love you much more than before. But God help me! it takes thee the more out of my reach!'

As they left the room to go to the audience with Cromwell, Katharine, squaring the frills of her hood behind her back, could hear Margot Poins grumbling to the magister:

'After these long days ye ha' time for five minutes to hold my hand,' and the magister, perturbed and fumbling in his bosom, muttered:

'Nay, I have no minutes now. I must write much in Latin ere thy mistress return.'

VI

'By God,' Wriothesley said when she entered the long gallery where the men were. 'This is a fair woman!'

She had command of her features, and her eyes were upon the ground; it was a part of a woman's upbringing to walk well, and her masters had so taught her when she had lived with her grandmother, the old duchess. Not the tips of her shoes shewed beneath the zigzag folds of her russet-brown underskirt; the tips of her scarlet sleeves netted with gold touched the waxed wood of the floor; her hood fell behind to the ground, and her fair hair was golden where the sunlight fell on it with a last, watery ray.

Upon Privy Seal she raised her eyes; she bent her knees so that her gown spread out all around her when she curtsied, and, having arranged it with a slow hand, she came to her height again, rustling as if she rose from a wave.

'Sir,' she said, 'I come to pray you to right a great wrong done by your servants.'

'By God!' Wriothesley said, 'she speaks high words.'

'Madam Howard,' Cromwell answered—and his eyes graciously dwelt upon her tall form. She had clasped her hands before her lap and looked into his face. 'Madam Howard, you are more learned in the better letters than I; but I would have you call to memory one Pancrates, of whom telleth Lucian. Being in a desert or elsewhere, this magician could turn sticks, stocks and stakes into servants that did his will. Mark you, they did his will—no more and no less.'

'Sir,' Katharine said, 'ye have better servants than ever had Pancrates. They do more than your behests.'

Cromwell bent his back, stretched aside his white hand and smiled still.

'Ye trow truth,' he said. 'Yet ye do me wrong; for had I the servants of Pancrates, assuredly he should hear no groans of injustice from men of good will.'

'It is too good hearing,' Katharine said gravely. 'This is my tale——'

Once before she had trembled in this man's presence, and still she had a catching in the throat as her eyes measured his face. She was mad to do right and to right wrongs, yet in his presence the doing of the right, the righting of wrongs, seemed less easy than when she stood before any other man. 'Sir,' she uttered, 'I have thought ye have done ill afore now. I am nowise certain that ye thought your ill-doing an evil. I beseech you for a patient hearing.'

But, though she told her story well—and it was an old story that she had learned by heart—she could not be rid of the feeling that this was a less easy matter than it had seemed to her, to call Cromwell accursed. She had a moving tale of wrongs done by Cromwell's servant, Dr Barnes, a visitor of a church in Lincolnshire near where her home had been. For the lands had been taken from a little priory upon an excuse that the nuns lived a lewd life; and so well had she known the nuns, going in and out of the convent every week-day, that well she knew the falseness of Cromwell's servant's tale.

'Sir,' she said to Cromwell, 'mine own foster-sister had the veil there; mine own mother's sister was there the abbess.' She stretched out a hand. 'Sir, they dwelled there simply and godly, withdrawn from the world; succouring the poor; weaving of fine linens, for much flax grew upon those lands by there; and praying God and the saints that blessings fall upon this land.'

Wriothesley spoke to her slowly and heavily:

'Such little abbeys ate up the substance of this land in the old days. Well have we prospered since they were done away who ate up the fatness of this realm. Now husbandmen till their idle soil and cattle are in their buildings.'

'Gentleman whose name I know not,' she turned upon him, 'more wealth and prosperity God granted us in answer to their prayers than could be won by all the husbandmen of Arcadia and all the kine of Cacus. God standeth above all men's labours.' But Cromwell's servants had sworn away the lands of the small abbey, and now the abbess and her nuns lay in gaol accused—and falsely—of having secreted an image of Saint Hugh to pray against the King's fortunes.

'Before God,' she said, 'and as Christ is my Saviour, I saw and make deposition that these poor simple women did no such thing but loved the King as he had been their good father. I have seen them at their prayers. Before God, I say to you that they were as folk astonished and dismayed; knowing so little of the world that ne one ne other knew whence came the word that had bared them to the skies. I have seen them—I.'

'Where went they?' Wriothesley said; 'what worked they?'

'Gentleman,' she answered; 'being cast out of their houses and their veils, they knew nowhither to go; homes they had none; they lived with their own hinds in hovels, like frightened lambs, the saints their pastors being driven from their folds.'

'Aye,' Wriothesley said grimly, 'they cumbered the ground; they did meet in knots for mutinies.'

'God had appointed them the duty of prayer,' Katharine answered him. 'They met and prayed in sheds and lodges of the house that had been theirs, poor ghosts revisiting and bewailing their earthly homes. I have prayed with them.'

'Ye have done a treason in that day,' Wriothesley answered.

'I have done the best that ever I did for this land,' she met him fully. 'I prayed naught against the King and the republic. I have prayed you and your like might be cast down. So do I still. I stand here to avow it. But they never did, and they do lie in gaol.' She turned again upon Cromwell and spoke piteously from her full throat. 'My lord,' she cried. 'Soften your heart and let the wax in your ears melt so that ye hear. Your servants swore falsely when they said these women lived lewdly; your men swore falsely when they said that these women prayed treasonably. For the one count they took their lands and houses; for the other they lay them in the gaols. Sir, my lord, your servants go up and down this land; sir, my lord, they ride rich men with boots of steel and do strangle the poor with gloves of iron. I do think ye know they do it; I do pray ye know not. But, sir, if ye will right this wrong I will kiss your hands; if you will set up again these homes of prayer I will take a veil, and in one of them spend my days praying that good befall you and yours.' She paused in her speaking and then began again: 'Before I came here I had made me a fair speech. I have forgot it, and words come haltingly to me. Sirs, ye think I seek mine own aggrandisement; ye think I do wish ye cast down. Before God, I wish ye were cast down if ye continue in these ways; but I have prayed to God who sent the Pentecostal fires, to give me the gift of tongues that shall soften your hearts——'

Cromwell interrupted her, smiling that Venus, who made her so fair, gave her no need of a gift of tongues, and Minerva, who made her so learned, gave her no need of fairness. For the sake of the one and the other, he would very diligently enquire into these women's courses. If they ha been guiltless, they should be richly repaid; if they ha been guilty, they should be pardoned.

Katharine flushed with a hot anger.

'Ye are a very craven lord,' she said. 'If you may find them guilty, you shall have my head. But if you do find them innocent and shield them not, I swear I will strive to have thine.' Anger made her blue eyes dilate. 'Have you no bowels of compassion for the right? Ye treat me as a fair woman—

but I speak as a messenger of the King's, that is God's, to men who too long have hardened their hearts.'

Throckmorton laid back his head and laughed suddenly at the ceiling; Cranmer crossed himself; Wriothesley beat his heel upon the floor and shrugged his shoulders bitterly—but Lascelles, the Archbishop's spy, kept his eyes upon Throckmorton's face with a puzzled scrutiny.

'Why now does that man laugh?' he asked himself. For it seemed to him that by laughing Throckmorton applauded Katharine Howard. And indeed, Throckmorton applauded Katharine Howard. As policy her speech was neither here nor there, but as voicing a spirit, infectious and winning to men's hearts, he saw that such speaking should carry her very far. And, if it should embroil her more than ever with Cromwell, it would the further serve his adventures. He was already conspiring to betray Cromwell, and he knew that, very soon now, Cromwell must pierce his mask of loyalty; and the more Katharine should have cast down her glove to Cromwell, the more he could shelter behind her; and the more men she could have made her friends with her beauty and her fine speeches, the more friends he too should have to his back when the day of discovery came. In the meantime he had in his sleeve a trick that he would speedily play upon Cromwell, the most dangerous of any that he had played. For below the stairs he had Udal, with his news of the envoy from Cleves to France, and with his copies of the envoy's letters. But, in her turn, Katharine played him, unwittingly enough, a trick that puzzled him.

'Bones of St Nairn!' he said; 'she has him to herself. What mad prank will she play now?'

Katharine had drawn Cromwell to the very end of the gallery.

'As I pray that Christ will listen to my pleas when at the last I come to Him for pardon and comfort,' she said, 'I swear that I will speak true words to you.'

He surveyed her, plump, alert, his lips moving one upon the other. He brought one white soft hand from behind his back to play with the furs upon his chest.

'Why, I believe you are a very earnest woman,' he said.

'Then, sir,' she said, 'understand that your sun is near its setting. We rise, we wane; our little days do run their course. But I do believe you love your King his cause more than most men.'

'Madam Howard,' he said, 'you have been my foremost foe.'

'Till five minutes agone I was,' she said.

He wondered for a moment if she were minded to beg him to aid her in growing to be Queen; and he wondered too how that might serve his turn. But she spoke again:

'You have very well served the King,' she said. 'You have made him rich and potent. I believe ye have none other desire so great as that desire to make him potent and high in this world's gear.'

'Madam Howard,' he said calmly, 'I desire that—and next to found for myself a great house that always shall serve the throne as well as I.'

She gave him the right to that with a lowering of her eyebrows.

'I too would see him a most high prince,' she said. 'I would see him shed lustre upon his friends, terror upon his foes, and a great light upon this realm and age.'

She paused to touch him earnestly with one long hand, and to brush back a strand of her hair. Down the gallery she saw Lascelles moving to speak with Throckmorton and Wriothesley holding the Archbishop earnestly by the sleeve.

'See,' she said, 'you are surrounded now by traitors that will bring you down. In foreign lands your cause wavers. I tell you, five minutes agone I wished you swept away.'

Cromwell raised his eyebrows.

'Why, I knew that this was difficult fighting,' he said. 'But I know not what giveth me your good wishes.'

'My lord,' she answered, 'it came to me in my mind: What man is there in the land save Privy Seal that so loveth his master's cause?'

Cromwell laughed.

'How well do you love this King,' he said.

'I love this King; I love this land,' she said, 'as Cato loved Rome or Leonidas his realm of Sparta.'

Cromwell pondered, looking down at his foot; his lips moved furtively, he folded his hand inside his sleeves; and he shook his head when again she made to speak. He desired another minute for thought.

'This I perceive to be the pact you have it in your mind to make,' he said at last, 'that if you come to sway the King towards Rome I shall still stay his man and yours?'

She looked at him, her lips parted with a slight surprise that he should so well have voiced thoughts that she had hardly put into words. Then her faith rose in her again and moved her to pitiful earnestness.

'My lord,' she uttered, and stretched out one hand. 'Come over to us. 'Tis such great pity else—'tis such pity else.'

She looked again at Throckmorton, who, in the distance, was surveying the Archbishop's spy with a sardonic amusement, and a great mournfulness went through her. For there was the traitor and here before her was the betrayed. Throckmorton had told her enough to know that he was conspiring against his master, and Cromwell trusted Throckmorton before any man in the land; and it was as if she saw one man with a dagger hovering behind another. With her woman's instinct she felt that the man about to die was the better man, though he were her foe. She was minded—she was filled with a great desire to say: 'Believe no word that Throckmorton shall tell you. The Duke of Cleves is now abandoning your cause.' That much she had learnt from Udal five minutes before. But she could not bring herself to betray Throckmorton, who was a traitor for the sake of her cause. ''Tis such pity,' she repeated again.

'Good wench,' Cromwell said, 'you are indifferent honest; but never while I am the King's man shall the Bishop of Rome take toll again in the King's land.'

She threw up her hands.

'Alack!' she said, 'shall not God and His Son our Saviour have their part of the King's glory?'

'God is above us all,' he answered. 'But there is no room for two heads of a State, and in a State is room but for one army. I will have my King so strong that ne Pope ne priest ne noble ne people shall here have speech or power. So it is now; I have so made it, the King helping me. Before I came this was a distracted State; the King's writ ran not in the east, not in the west, not in the north, and hardly in the south parts. Now no lord nor no bishop nor no Pope raises head against him here. And, God willing, in all the world no prince shall stand but by grace of this King's Highness. This land shall have the wealth of all the world; this King shall guide this land. There shall be rich husbandmen paying no toll to priests, but to the King alone; there shall be wealthy merchants paying no tax to any prince nor emperor, but only to this King. The King's court shall redress all wrongs; the King's voice shall be omnipotent in the council of the princes.'

'Ye speak no word of God,' she said pitifully.

'God is very far away,' he answered.

'Sir, my lord,' she cried, and brushed again the tress from her forehead. 'Ye have made this King rich with gear of the Church: if ye will be friends with me ye shall make this King a pauper to repay; ye have made this King stiffen his neck against God's Vicegerent: if you and I shall work together ye shall make him re-humble himself. Christ the King of all the world was a pauper; Christ the Saviour of all mankind humbled Himself before God that was His Saviour.'

Cromwell said 'Amen.'

'Sir,' she said again; 'ye have made this King rich, but I will give to him again his power to sleep at night; ye have made this realm subject to this King, but, by the help of God, I will make it subject again to God. You have set up here a great State, but oh, the children of God do weep since ye came. Where is a town where lamentation is not heard? Where is a town where no orphan or widow bewails the day that saw your birth?' She had sobs in her voice and she wrung her hands. 'Sir,' she cried, 'I say you are as a dead man already—your day of pride is past, whether ye aid us or no. Set yourself then to redress as heartily as ye have set yourself in the past to make sad. That land is blest whose people are happy; that State is aggrandised whence there arise songs praising God for His blessings. You have built up a great city of groans; set yourself now to build a kingdom where "Praise God" shall be sung. It is a contented people that makes a State great; it is the love of God that maketh a people rich.'

Cromwell laughed mirthlessly:

'There are forty thousand men like Wriothesley in England,' he said. 'God help you if you come against them; there are forty times forty thousand and forty times that that pray you not again to set disorder loose in this land. I have broken all stiff necks in this realm. See you that you come not against some yet.' He stopped, and added: 'Your greatest foes should be your own friends if I be a dead man as you say.' And he smiled at her bewilderment when he had added: 'I am your bulwark and your safeguard.'

... 'For, listen to me,' he took up again his parable. 'Whilst I be here I bear the rancour of your friends' hatred. When I am gone you shall inherit it.'

'Sir,' she said, 'I am not here to hear riddles, but here I am to pray you seek the right.'

'Wench,' he said pleasantly, 'there are in this world many rights—you have yours; I mine. But mine can never be yours nor yours mine. I am not yet so dead as ye say; but if I be dead, I wish you so well that I will send you a phial of poison ere I send to take you to the stake. For it is certain that if you have not my head I shall have yours.'

She looked at him seriously, though the tears ran down her cheeks.

'Sir,' she uttered, 'I do take you to be a man of your word. Swear to me, then, that if upon the fatal hill I do save you your life and your estates, you will nowise work the undoing of the Church in time to come.'

'Madam Queen that shall be,' he said, 'an ye gave me my life this day, to-morrow I would work as I worked yesterday. If ye have faith of your cause I have the like of mine.'

She hung her head, and said at last:

'Sir, an ye have a little door here at the gallery end I will go out by it'; for she would not again face the men who made the little knot before the window. He moved the hangings aside and stood before the aperture smiling.

'Ye came to ask a boon of me,' he said. 'Is it your will still that I grant it?'

'Sir,' she answered, 'I asked a boon of you that I thought you would not grant, so that I might go to the King and shew him your evil dealings with his lieges.'

'I knew it well,' he said. 'But the King will not cast me down till the King hath had full use of me.'

'You have a very great sight into men's minds,' she uttered, and he laughed noiselessly once again.

'I am as God made me,' he said. Then he spoke once more. 'I will read your mind if you will. Ye came to me in this crisis, thinking with yourself: *Liars go unto the King saying, "This Cromwell is a traitor; cast him down, for he seeks your ill." I will go unto the King saying, "This Cromwell grindeth the faces of the poor and beareth false witness. Cast him down, though he serve you well, since he maketh your name to stink to heaven."* So I read my fellow-men.'

'Sir,' she said, 'it is very true that I will not be linked with liars. And it is very true that men do so speak of you to the King's Highness.'

'Why,' he answered her debonairly, 'the King shall listen neither to them nor to you till the day be come. Then he will act in his own good way— upon the pretext that I be a traitor, or upon the pretext that I have borne false witness, or upon no pretext at all.'

'Nevertheless will I speak for the truth that shall prevail,' she answered.

'Why, God help you!' was his rejoinder.

Going back to his friends in the window Cromwell meditated that it was possible to imagine a woman that thought so simply; yet it was impossible to imagine one that should be able to act with so great a simplicity. On the one hand, if she stayed about the King she should be his safeguard, for it was very certain that she should not tell the King that he was a traitor. And that above all was what Cromwell had to fear. He had, for his own purposes, so filled the King with the belief that treachery overran his land, that the King saw treachery in every man. And Cromwell was aware, well enough, that such of his adherents as were Protestant—such men as Wriothesley—had indeed boasted that they were twenty thousand swords ready to fall upon even the King if he set against the re-forming religion in England. This was the greatest danger that he had—that an enemy of his should tell the King that Privy Seal had behind his back twenty thousand swords. For that side of the matter Katharine Howard was even a safeguard, since with her love of truth she would assuredly combat these liars with the King.

But, on the other hand, the King had his superstitious fears; only that night, pale, red-eyed and heavy, and being unable to sleep, he had sent to rouse Cromwell and had furiously rated him, calling him knave and shaking him by the shoulder, telling him for the twentieth time to find a way to make a peace with the Bishop of Rome. These were only night-fears—but, if Cleves should desert Henry and Protestantism, if all Europe should stand solid for the Pope, Henry's night-fears might eat up his day as well. Then indeed Katharine would be dangerous. So that she was indeed half foe, half friend.

It hinged all upon Cleves; for if Cleves stood friend to Protestantism the King would fear no treason; if Cleves sued for pardon to the Emperor and Rome, Henry must swing towards Katharine. Therefore, if Cleves stood firm to Protestantism and defied the Emperor, it would be safe to work at destroying Katharine; if not, he must leave her by the King to defend his very loyalty.

The Archbishop challenged him with uplifted questioning eyebrows, and he answered his gaze with:

'God help ye, goodman Bishop; it were easier for thee to deal with this maid than for me. She would take thee to her friend if thou wouldst curry with Rome.'

'Aye,' Cranmer answered. 'But would Rome have truck with me?' and he shook his head bitterly. He had been made Archbishop with no sanction from Rome.

Cromwell turned upon Wriothesley; the debonair smile was gone from his face; the friendly contempt that he had for the Archbishop was gone too; his eyes were hard, cruel and red, his lips hardened.

'Ye have done me a very evil turn,' he said. 'Ye spoke stiff-necked folly to this lady. Ye shall learn, Protestants that ye are, that if I be the flail of the monks I may be a hail, a lightning, a bolt from heaven upon Lutherans that cross the King.'

The hard malice of his glance made Wriothesley quail and flush heavily.

'I thought ye had been our friend,' he said.

'Wriothesley,' Cromwell answered, 'I tell thee, silly knave, that I be friend only to them that love the order and peace I have made, under the King's Highness, in this realm. If it be the King's will to stablish again the old faith, a hammer of iron will I be upon such as do raise their heads against it. It were better ye had never been born, it were better ye were dead and asleep, than that ye raised your heads against me.' He turned, then he swung back with the sharpness of a viper's spring.

'What help have I had of thee and thy friends? I have bolstered up Cleves and his Lutherans for ye. What have he and ye done for me and my King? Your friend the Duke of Cleves has an envoy in Paris. Have ye found for why he comes there? Ye could not. Ye have botched your errand to Paris; ye have spoken naughtily in my house to a friend of the King's that came friendlily to me.' He shook a fat finger an inch from Wriothesley's eyes. 'Have a care! I did send my visitors to smell out treason among the convents and abbeys. Wait ye till I send them to your conventicles! Ye shall not scape. Body of God! ye shall not scape.'

He placed a heavy hand upon Throckmorton's shoulder.

'I would I had sent thee to Paris,' he said. 'No envoy had come there whose papers ye had not seen. I warrant thou wouldst have ferreted them through.'

Throckmorton's eyes never moved; his mouth opened and he spoke with neither triumph nor malice:

'In very truth, Privy Seal,' he said, 'I have ferreted through enow of them to know why the envoy came to Paris.'

Cromwell kept his hands still firm upon his spy's shoulder whilst the swift thoughts ran through his mind. He scowled still upon Wriothesley.

'Sir,' he said, 'ye see how I be served. What ye could not find in Paris my man found for me in London town.' He moved his face round towards the great golden beard of his spy. 'Ye shall have the farms ye asked me for in

Suffolk,' he said. 'Tell me now wherefore came the Cleves envoy to France. Will Cleves stay our ally, or will he send like a coward to his Emperor?'

'Privy Seal,' Throckmorton answered expressionlessly—he fingered his beard for a moment and felt at the medal depending upon his chest— 'Cleves will stay your friend and the King's ally.'

A great sigh went up from his three hearers at Throckmorton's lie; and impassive as he was, Throckmorton sighed too, imperceptibly beneath the mantle of his beard. He had burned his boats. But for the others the sigh was of a great contentment. With Cleves to lead the German Protestant confederation, the King felt himself strong enough to make headway against the Pope, the Emperor and France. So long as the Duke of Cleves remained a rebel against his lord the Emperor, the King would hold over Protestantism the mantle of his protection.

Cromwell broke in upon their thoughts with his swift speech.

'Sirs,' he uttered, 'then what ye will shall come to pass. Wriothesley, I pardon thee; get thee back to Paris to thy mission. Archbishop, I trow thou shalt have the head of that wench. Her cousin shall be brought here again from France.'

Lascelles, the Archbishop's spy, who kept his gaze upon Throckmorton's, saw the large man's eyes shift suddenly from one board of the floor to another.

'That man is not true,' he said to himself, and fell into a train of musing. But from the others Cromwell had secured the meed of wonder that he desired. He had closed the interview with a dramatic speech; he had given them something to talk of.

VII

He held Throckmorton in the small room that contained upon its high stand the Privy Seal of England in an embroidered purse. All red and gold, this symbol of power held the eye away from the dark-green tapestry and from the pigeon-holes filled with parchment scrolls wherefrom there depended so many seals each like a gout of blood. The room was so high that it appeared small, but there was room for Cromwell to pace about, and here, walking from wall to wall, he evolved those schemes that so fast held down the realm. He paced always, his hands behind his back, his lips moving one upon the other as if he ruminated—(His foes said that he talked thus with his familiar fiend that had the form of a bee.)—and his black cap with ear-flaps always upon his head, for he suffered much with the earache.

He walked now, up and down and up and down, saying nothing, whilst from time to time Throckmorton spoke a word or two. Throckmorton himself had his doubts—doubts as to how the time when it would be safe to let it be known that he had betrayed his master might be found to fit in with the time when his master must find that he had betrayed him. He had, as he saw it, to gain time for Katharine Howard so she might finally enslave the King's desires. That there was one weak spot in her armour he thought he knew, and that was her cousin that was said to be her lover. That Cromwell knew of her weak spot he knew too; that Cromwell through that would strike at her he knew too. All depended upon whether he could gain time so that Cromwell should be down before he could use his knowledge.

For that reason he had devised the scheme of making Cromwell feel a safety about the affairs of Cleves. Udal fortunately wrote a very swift Latin. Thus, when going to fetch Katharine to her interview with Privy Seal he had found Udal bursting with news of the Cleves embassy and with the letters of the Duke of Cleves actually copied on papers in his poke, Throckmorton had very swiftly advised with himself how to act. He had set Udal very earnestly to writing a false letter from Cleves to France—such a letter as Cleves might have written—and this false letter, in the magister's Latin, he had placed now in his master's hands, and, pacing up and down, Cromwell read from time to time from the scrap of paper.

What Cleves had written was that he was fain to make submission to the Emperor, and leave the King's alliance. What Cromwell read was this: That the high and mighty Prince, the Duke of Cleves, was firmly minded to adhere in his allegiance with the King of England: that he feared the wrath of the Emperor Charles, who was his very good suzerain and over-lord: that if by taxes and tributes he might keep away from his territory the armies of the Emperor he would be well content to pay a store of gold: that he begged his friend and uncle, King of France, to intercede betwixt himself and the Emperor to the end that the Emperor might take these taxes and tributes; for that, if the Emperor would none of this, come peace, come war, he, the high and mighty Prince, Duke of Cleves, Elector of the Empire, was minded to protect in Germany the Protestant confession and to raise against the Emperor the Princes and Electors of Almain, being Protestants. With the aid of his brother-in-law the King of England he would drive the Emperor Charles from the German lands together with the heresies of the Romish Bishop and all things that pertained to the Emperor Charles and his religion.

Cromwell had listened to the reading of this letter in silence; in silence he re-perused it himself, pacing up and down, and in between phrases of his thoughts he read passages from it and nodded his head.

That this was a very dangerous enterprise Throckmorton was assured; it was the first overt act of his that Privy Seal could discover in him as a treachery. In a month or six weeks he must know the truth; but in a month or six weeks Katharine must have so enslaved the King that all danger from Cromwell would be past. And he trusted that the security that Cromwell must feel would gar him delay striking at Katharine by means of her cousin.

Cromwell said suddenly:

'How got the magister these papers?' and Throckmorton answered that it was through the widow that kept the tavern. Cromwell said negligently:

'Let the magister be rewarded with ten crowns a quarter to his fees. Set it down in my tables'; and then like lightning came the query:

'Do ye believe of her cousin and the Lady Katharine?'

Craving a respite for thought and daring to take none for fear Cromwell should read him, Throckmorton answered:

'Ye know I think yes.'

'I have said I think no,' Cromwell answered in turn, but dispassionately as though it were a matter of the courses of stars; 'though it is very certain that her cousin is so mad with love for her that we had much ado to send him from her to Paris.' He paced three times from wall to wall and then spoke again:

'Men enow have said she was too fond with her cousin?'

With despair in his heart Throckmorton answered:

'It is the common talk in Lincolnshire where her home is. I have seen a cub in a cowherd's that was said to be her child by him.'

It was useless to speak otherwise to Privy Seal; if he did not report these things, twenty others would. But, beneath his impassive face and his great beard, despair filled him. He might swear treason against Cromwell to the King; but the King would not hear him alone, and without the King and Katharine he was a sparrow in Cromwell's hawk's talons.

'Why,' Cromwell said, 'since Cleves is true to us we will have this woman down. An he had played us false I would have kept her near the King.'

This saying, that ran so counter to Throckmorton's schemes, caused him such dismay that he cried out:

'God forgive us, why?'

Cromwell smiled at him as one who smiles from a great height, and pointed a finger.

'This is a hard fight,' he said; 'we are in some straits. I trow ye would have voiced it otherwise.' And then he voiced his own idea—that so long as Cleves was friends with him Katharine was an enemy; if Cleves fell away she was none the less an enemy, but she would, from her love of justice, bear witness to the King that Cromwell was no traitor. 'And ye shall be very certain,' he added pleasantly, 'that once men see the King so inclined, they will go to the King saying I be a traitor, with Protestants like Wriothesley ready to rise and aid me. In that pass the Lady Katharine should stay by me, in the King's ear.'

A deep and intolerable dejection overcame Throckmorton and forced from his lips the words:

'Ye reason most justly.' And again he cursed himself, for he had forced Cromwell to this reasoning and action. Yet he dared not say that his news of the Cleves embassy was false, that Cleves indeed was minded to turn traitor, and that it most would serve Privy Seal's turn to stay Katharine Howard up. He dared not say the words, yet he saw his safety crumbling, and he saw Privy Seal set to ruin both himself and Katharine Howard. For in his heart he could not believe that the woman was virtuous, since he believed that no woman was virtuous who had been given the opportunity for joyment. As a spy, he had gone nosing about in Lincolnshire where Katharine's home had been near her cousin's. He had heard many tales against her such as rustics will tell against the daughters of poor lords like Katharine's father. And these tales, before ever he had come to love her, he had set down in Privy Seal's private registers. Now they were like to undo him and her. And in truth, according to his premonitions, Cromwell spoke:

'We shall bring very quickly Thomas Culpepper, her cousin, back from France. We shall inflame his mind with jealousy of the King. We shall find a place where he shall burst upon the King and her together. We shall bring witnesses enow from Lincolnshire to swear against her.'

He crossed his hands behind his back.

'This work of fetching her cousin from Paris I will put into the hands of Viridus,' he said. 'I believe her to be virtuous, therefore do you bring many witnesses, and some that shall swear to have seen her in the act. That shall be your employment. For I tell you she hath so great a power of pleading that, being innocent, she will with difficulty be proved unchaste.'

Throckmorton's head hung upon his shoulders.

'Remember,' Privy Seal said again, 'you and Viridus shall send to find her cousin in France. Fill him with tales that his cousin plays the leman with the King. He shall burst here like a bolt from heaven. You will find him betwixt Calais and Paris town, dallying in evil places without a doubt. We sent him thither to frighten Cardinal Pole.'

'Aye,' Throckmorton said, his mind filled with other and bitter thoughts. 'He hath frightened the Cardinal from Paris by the mere renown of his violence.'

'Then let him do some frighting in our goodly town of London,' Cromwell said.

PART TWO
THE DISTANT CLOUD

I

The young Poins, once an ensign of the King's guard, habited now in grey, stood awaiting Thomas Culpepper, Katharine Howard's cousin, beneath the new gateway towards the east of Calais. Four days he had waited already and never had he dared to stir, save when the gates were closed for the night. But it had chanced that one of the gatewardens was a man from Lincolnshire—a man, once a follower of the plough, whose father had held a farm in the having of Culpepper himself.

'——But he sold 'un,' Nicholas Hogben said, 'sold 'un clear away.' He made a wry face, winked one eye, and drawing up the right corner of his mouth, displayed square, huge teeth. The young Poins making no question, he repeated twice: 'Clear away. Right clear away.'

Poins, however, could hold but one thing of a time in his head. And, by that striving, dangerous servant of Lord Privy Seal, Throckmorton, it had been firmly enjoined upon him that he must not fail to meet Thomas Culpepper and stay him upon his road to England. Throckmorton, with his great beard and cruel snake's eyes, had said: 'I hold thy head in fee. If ye would save it, meet Thomas Culpepper in Calais and give him this letter.' The letter he had in his poke. It carried with it a deed making Culpepper lieutenant of the stone barges in Calais. But he had it too, by word of mouth, that if Thomas Culpepper would not be stayed by the letter, he, Hal Poins, must stay him—with the sword, with a stab in the back, or by being stabbed himself and calling in the guard to lay Thomas Culpepper's self by the heels.

'You will enjoin upon him,' Throckmorton had said, 'how goodly a thing is the lieutenancy of stone lighters that in this letter is proffered him. You will tell him that, if a barge of stone go astray, it is yet a fair way to London, and stone fetches good money from townsmen building in Calais. If he will gainsay this you will pick a quarrel with him, as by saying he gives you the lie. In short,' Throckmorton had finished, earnestly and with a sinuous grace of gesture in his long and narrow hands, 'you will stay him.'

It was a desperate measure, yet it was the best he could compass. If Culpepper came to London, if he came to the King, Katharine's fortunes were not worth a rushlight such as were sold at twenty for a farthing. He knew, too, that Viridus had Cromwell's earnest injunctions to send a messenger that should hasten Culpepper's return; and, though he had seven hundred of Cromwell's spies that he could trust to do Privy Seal's errand, he had not one that he could trust to do his own. There was no one of them that he could trust. If he took a spy and said: 'At all costs stay Culpepper, but observe very strict secrecy from Privy Seal's men all,' the spy would very certainly let the news come to Privy Seal.

It was in this pass that the thought of the young Poins had come to him. Here was a fellow absolutely stupid. He was a brother of Katharine Howard's tiring maid who had already come near to losing his head in a former intrigue in the Court. He had, at the instigation of his sister, carried two Papist letters of Katharine Howard. And, if it was the King who pardoned him, it was Throckmorton who first had taken him prisoner; it was Throckmorton who had advised him to lie hidden in his grandfather's house for a month or two. At the time Throckmorton had had no immediate reason to give the boy this counsel. Poins had been so small a tool in the past embroilment of Katharine's letter that, had he gone straight back to his post in the yeomanry of the King's guard, no man would have noticed him. But it had always been part of the devious and great bearded man's policy—it had been part of his very nature—to play upon people's fears, to trouble them with apprehensions. It was part of the tradition that Cromwell had given all his men. He ruled England by such fears.

Thus Throckmorton had sent Poins trembling to hide in the old printer's his grandfather's house in the wilds of Austin Friars. And Throckmorton had impressed upon him that he alone had really saved him. It was in his grandfather's mean house that Poins had remained for a brace of months, grumbled at by his Protestant uncle and sneered at by his malicious Papist grandfather. And it was here that Throckmorton had found him, dressed in grey, humbled from his pride and raging for things to do.

The boy would be of little service—yet he was all that Throckmorton had. If he could hardly be expected to trick Culpepper with his tongue, he might wound him with his sword; if he could not kill him he might at least scotch him, cause a brawl in Calais town, where, because the place was an outpost, brawling was treason, and Culpepper might be had by the heels for long enough to let Cromwell fall. Therefore, in the low room with the black presses, in the very shadow of Cromwell's own walls, Throckmorton—who was given the privacy of the place by the Lutheran printer because he was Cromwell's man—large, golden-bearded and speaking in meaning whispers, with lifting of his eyebrows, had held a long conference with the lad.

His dangerous and terrifying presence seemed to dominate, for the young Poins, even the dusty archway of the Calais gate—and, even though he saw the flat, green and sunny levels of the French marshland, with the town of Ardres rising grey and turreted six miles away, the young Poins felt that he was still beneath the eyes of Throckmorton, the spy who had sought him out in his grandfather's house in Austin Friars to send him here across the seas to Calais. Up above in the archway the stonemasons who came from Lydd sang their Kentish songs as hammers clinked on chisels and the fine dust filtered through the scaffold boards. But the young Poins kept his eyes upon the dusty and winding road that threaded the dykes from Ardres, and thought only that when Thomas Culpepper came he must be stayed. He had oiled his sword that had been his father's so that it would slip smoothly from the scabbard; he had filed his dagger so that it would pierce through thin coat of mail. It was well to be armed, though he could not see why Thomas Culpepper should not stay willingly at Calais to be lieutenant of the stone lighters and steal stone to fill his pockets, since such were the privileges of the post that Throckmorton offered him.

'Mayhap, if I stay him, it will get me advancement,' he grumbled between his teeth. He was enraged in his slow, fierce way. For Throckmorton had promised him only to save his neck if he succeeded. There had been no hint of further rewards. He did not speculate upon why Thomas Culpepper was to be held in Calais; he did not speculate upon why he should wish to come to England; but again and again he muttered between his teeth, 'A curst business! a curst business!'

In the mysterious embroilment in which formerly he had taken part, his sister had told him that he was carrying letters between the King and Kat Howard. Yes; his large, slow sister had promised him great advancement for carrying certain letters. And still, in spite of the fact that he had been told it was a treason, he believed that the letters he had carried for Kat Howard were love letters to the King. Nevertheless, for his services he had received no advancement; he had, on the contrary, been bidden to leave his comrades of the guard and to hide himself. Throckmorton had bidden him do this. And instead of advancement, he had received kicks, curses, cords on his wrists, an interview with the Lord Privy Seal that still in the remembrance set him shivering, and this chance, offered him by Throckmorton, that if he stayed Thomas Culpepper he might save his neck.

'Why, then,' he grumbled to himself, 'is it treason to carry the King's letters to a wench? Helping the King is no treason. I should be advanced, not threatened with a halter. Letters between the King and Kat Howard!' He even attempted to himself a clumsy joke, polishing it and repolishing it till it came out: 'A King may write to a Kat. A Kat may write to a King. But my neck's in danger!'

Beside him, whitened by the dust that fell from above, the gatewarden wandered in speech round *his* grievance.

'You ask me, young lad, if I know Tom Culpepper. Well I know Tom Culpepper. Y' ask me if he have passed this way going for England. Well I know he have not. For if Tom Culpepper, squire that was of Durford and Maintree and Sallowford that was my father's farm—if so be Tom Culpepper had passed this way, I had spat in the dust behind him as he passed.'

He made his wry face, winked his eye and showed his teeth once more. 'Spat in the dust—I should ha' spat in the dust,' he remarked again. 'Or maybe I'd have cast my hat on high wi' "Huzzay, Squahre Tom!" according as the mood I was in,' he said. He winked again and waited.

'For sure,' he affirmed after a pause, 'that will move 'ee to ask why I du spit in the dust or for why—the thing being contrary—I'd ha' cast up my cap.'

The young Poins pulled an onion from his poke.

'If you are so main sure he have not passed the gate,' he said, 'I may take my ease.' He sat him down against the gate wall where the April sun fell warm through the arch of shadows. He stripped the outer peel from the onion and bit into it. 'Good, warming eating,' he said, 'when your stomach's astir from the sea.'

'Young lad,' the gatewarden said, 'I'm as fain to swear my mother bore me—though God forbid I should swear who my father was, woman being woman—as that Thomas Culpepper have not passed this way. For why: I'd have cast my hat on high or spat on the ground. And such things done mark other things that have passed in the mind of a man. And I have done no such thing.'

But because the young Poins sat always silent with his eyes on the road to Ardres and slept—being privileged because he was yeoman of the King's guard—always in the little stone guard cell of the gateway at nights; because, in fact, the young man's whole faculties were set upon seeing that Thomas Culpepper did not pass unseen through the gate, it was four days before the gatewarden contrived to get himself asked why he would have spat in the dust or cast his hat on high. It was, as it were, a point of honour that he should be asked for all the information that he gave; and he thirsted to tell his tale.

His tale had it that he had been ruined by a wench who had thrown her shoe over the mill and married a horse-smith, after having many times tickled the rough chin of Nicholas Hogben. Therefore, he had it that all women were to be humbled and held down—for all women were traitors, praters, liars, worms and vermin. (He made a great play of words between wermen, meaning worms, and wermin and wummin.) He had been ruined by this woman who had tickled him under the chin—that being an ingratiating act, fit to bewitch and muddle a man, like as if she had promised him marriage. And then she had married a horse-smith! So he was ready and willing, and prayed every night that God would send him the chance, to ruin and hold down every woman who walked the earth or lay in a bed.

But he had been ruined, too, by Thomas Culpepper, who had sold Durford and Maintree and Sallowford—which last was Hogben's father's farm. For why? Selling the farm had let in a Lincoln lawyer, and the Lincoln lawyer had set the farm to sheep, which last had turned old Hogben, the father, out from his furrows to die in a ditch—there being no room for farmers and for sheep upon one land. It had sent old Hogben, the father, to die in a ditch; it had sent his daughters to the stews and his sons to the road for sturdy beggars. So that, but for Wallop's band passing that way when Hogben was grinning through the rope beneath Lincoln town tree—but for the fact that men were needed for Wallop's work in Calais, by the holy blood of Hailes! Hogben would have been rating the angel's head in Paradise.

But there had been great call for men to man the walls there in Calais, so Wallop's ancient had written his name down on the list, beneath the gallows tree, and had taken him away from the Sheriff of Lincoln's man.

'So here a be,' he drawled, 'cutting little holes in my pikehead.'

''Tis a folly,' the young Poins said.

'Sir,' the Lincolnshire man answered, 'you say 'tis a folly to make small holes in a pikehead. But for me 'tis the greatest of ornaments. Give you, it weakens the pikehead; but 'tis a gradely ornament.'

'Ornaments be folly,' the young Poins reiterated.

'Sir,' the Lincolnshire man answered again, 'there is the goodliest folly that ever was. For if I weaken my eyes and tire my wrists with small tappers and little files, and if I weaken the steel with small holes, each hole represents a woman I have known undone and cast down in her pride by a man. Here be sixty-and-four holes round and firm in a pattern. Sixty-and-four women I have known undone.'

He paused and surveyed, winking and moving the scroll that the little holes made in the tough steel of his axehead. Where a perforation was not quite round, he touched it with his file.

'Hum! ha!' he gloated. 'In the centre of the head is the master hole of all, planned out for being cut. But not yet cut! Mark you, 'tis not yet cut. That is for the woman I hate most of all women. She is not yet cast down that I have heard tell on, though some have said "Aye," some "Nay." Tell me, have you heard yet of a Kat Howard in the stews?'

'There is a Kat Howard is like to be——' the young Poins began. But his slow cunning was aroused before he had the sentence out. Who could tell what trick was this?

'Like to be what?' the Lincolnshire man badgered him. 'Like to be what? To be what?'

'Nay, I know not,' Poins answered.

'Like to be what?' Hogben persisted.

'I know no Kat Howard,' Poins muttered sulkily. For he knew well that the Lady Katharine's name was up in the taverns along of Thomas Culpepper. And this Lincolnshire cow-dog was a knave too of Thomas's; therefore the one Kat Howard who was like to be the King's wench and the other Kat Howard known to Hogben might well be one and the same.

'Nay; if you will not, neither even will I,' Hogben said. 'You shall have no more of my tale.'

Poins kept his blue eyes along the road. Far away, with an odd leap, waving its arms abroad and coming by fits and starts, as a hare gambols along a path—a figure was tiny to see, coming from Ardres way towards Calais. It passed a load of hay on an ox-cart, and Poins could see the peasants beside it scatter, leap the dyke and fly to stand panting in the fields. The figure was clenching its fists; then it fell to kicking the oxen; when they had overset the cart into the dyke, it came dancing along with the same hare's gait.

'That is too like the repute of Thomas Culpepper to be other than Thomas Culpepper,' the young Poins said. 'I will go meet him.'

He started to his feet, loosed the sword in its scabbard; but the Lincolnshire man had his halberd across the gateway.

'Pass! Shew thy pass!' he said vindictively.

'I go but to meet him,' Poins snarled.

'A good lie; thou goest not,' Hogben answered. 'No Englishman goes into the French lands without a pass from the lord controller. An thou keepest a shut head I can e'en keep a shut gate.'

None the less he must needs talk or stifle.

'Thee, with thy Kat Howard,' he snarled. 'Would 'ee have me think thy Kat was my kitten whose name stunk in our nostrils?'

He shook his finger in Poins' face.

'Here be three of us know Kat Howard,' he said. 'For I know her, since for her I must leave home and take the road. And *he* knoweth her over well or over ill, since, to buy her a gown, he sold the three farms, Maintree, Durford and Sallowford—which last was my father's farm. And *thee* knowest her. Thee knowest her. To no good, I'se awarned. For thou stoppedst in thy speech like a colt before a wood snake. God bring down all women, I pray!'

He went on to tell, as if it had been a rosary, the names of the ruined women that the holes in his pikehead represented. There was one left by the wayside with her child; there was one hung for stealing cloth to cover her; there was one whipped for her naughty ways. He reached the square mark in the centre as the figure on the road reached the gateway.

'Huzzay, Squahre Tom! Here bay three kennath Kat Howard. Let us three tak part to kick her down.'

Thomas Culpepper like a green cat flew at his throat, clutched him above the steel breastplate, and shook three times, the gatewarden's uncovered, dun-coloured head swaying back and forward as if it were a loose bundle of clouts on a mop. When they parted company, because he could no longer keep his fingers clenched, Hogben fell back; he fell back, and they lay with their heels touching each other and their arms stretched out in the dust.

II

Nicholas Hogben was the first to rise. He felt at his neck, swallowed as though a piece of apple were stuck in his throat, brushed his leather breeches, and picked up his pike.

'Why,' he said, 'you may hold it for main and certain that he have not had Kat Howard down. For, having had her down, a would never have thrown a man by the throat for miscalling of her. Therefore Kat Howard is up for all of he, and I may loosen my feelings.'

He spat gravely at Culpepper's feet. Culpepper lay in the dust, his arms stretched out to form a cross, his face dead white and his beard of brilliant red pointing at the keystone of the arch of Calais gate. Poins lifted his hand, but the pulse still beat, and he dropped it moodily in the dust.

'Not dead,' he muttered.

'Dead!' Hogben laughed at him. 'Hath been in a boosing ken. There they drug the wine with simples, and the women—may pox fall on all women—perfume themselves so that a man goeth stark raving. I warrant he had silver buttons to his Lincoln green, but they be torn off. I warrant he had gold buckles to his shoen, but they be gone. His sword is away, the leather hangers being cut.'

'Wilt not stick him with thy pike, having, as he hath, so mishandled thee?'

'O aye,' the Lincolnshire man shewed his strong teeth. 'Thee wouldst have Kat Howard from him. But he may live for me, being more like to bring her to dismay than ever thee wilt be!'

He looked into the narrow street of the town that the dawn pierced into through the gateway. Two skinny men in jerkins drawn tight with belts were yawning in a hovel's low doorway. Under his eyes, still stretching their arms abroad, they made to slink between the mud walls of the next alley.

'Oh, hi! *Arrestez. Vesnez!* he hailed. '*Cestui à comforter!* The thin men made to break away, halted, hesitated, and then with dragging feet made through the pools and filth to the gateway.

'*Tombé! Voleurs! Secourez!* Hogben pointed at the prostrate figure in green. They rubbed their shins on their thin calves and appeared bewildered and uncertain.

'*Portez à lous maisons!* Hogben commanded.

They stood one on each side and bent down, extending skinny arms to lift him. Thomas Culpepper sat up and spat in their faces—they fled like scared wolves, noiselessly, gazing behind them in trepidation.

'Stay them; thieves ho! Stay them!' Culpepper panted. He scrambled to his feet, and stood reeling, his face like death, when he tried to make after them.

'God!' he said. 'Give me to drink.'

The young Poins mused under his breath because the man had neither sword nor dagger. Therefore it would be impossible to have sword play with him. He had, the young man, no ferocity—but he was set there to stay Thomas Culpepper's going on to England; he was to stay him by word or by deed. Deeds came so much easier than words.

'Squahre Tom!' the Lincolnshire man grunted. 'Reckon you have no money. Without groats and more ye shall get nowt to drink in Calais town, save water. Water you may have in plenty.'

With a sigh the young Poins unbuckled his belt to get his papers.

'Money I have for you,' he said. 'A main of money.' He was engaged now to pass words with this man—and he sighed again.

But Thomas Culpepper disregarded his words and his sigh. He was more in the mood to talk Lincolnshire than Kent, for his fever had given him a touch of homesickness and the young Poins to him was a very foreigner. He shut his eyes to let the Lincolnshire gatewarden's words go down to his brain; then with sudden violence he spat out:

'Give me water! What do ah ask but water! Pig! brood of a sow! gi'e me water and choke!'

Nicholas Hogben fetched a leather bottle as long as his leg, dusty and dinted, but nevertheless bedight with the arms of England, from the stone recess where the guard sheltered at nights. He fitted it on to the crook of his pike by the handle, and, craning over the drawbridge, first smoothed away the leaf-green duck-weed on the moat and then sank the bottle in the black water.

'I have money: a main of money for ye,' the young Poins said to Thomas Culpepper; but the man, with his red beard and white face, swayed on his legs and had ears only for the gurgling and gulping of the water as it entered the bottle neck. The black jack swayed and jumped below the bridge like a glistening water-beast.

He had little green spangles of duck-weed in his orange beard when he took the bottle away, empty, from his mouth. He drew deep gasps of breath, and suddenly sat down upon a squared block of stone that the masons above were waiting to hoist into place over the archway.

'Good water!' he grunted to Hogben—grunting as all the Lincolnshire men did, in those days, like a two-year hog.

'Bean't but that good in all Calais town!' Hogben grunted back to him. 'Curses on the two wurmen that sent me here.' And indeed, to Lincolnshire men the water tasted good, since it reminded them of their dyke water, tasting of marshweed and smelling of eggs.

'Tü wurmen!' Culpepper said lazily. 'Hast thou been jigging with *tü* puticotties to wunst? One is enow to undo seven men. Who be 'hee?'

The young Poins, with a sulky sense of his importance, uttered:

'I have money for thee—a main of money!'

Culpepper looked at him with sleepy blue eyes.

'Thrice y' ha' told me that,' he said. 'And money is a goodly thing in its place—but not to a man with a bellyful of water. Y' shall feel my fist when I be rested. Meanwhile wait and, being a cub, hear how *men* talk.' He slapped his chest and repeated to Hogben: 'Who be 'ee?'

Hogben, delighted to be asked at last a question, shewed his formidable teeth and beneath his familiar contortion of the eyelids brought out the words that one of the women who had brought him down was her that had brought Squahre Culpepper to sit on a squared stone before Calais gate.

'Why, I am a made man, for all you see me sit here,' Culpepper answered indolently. 'I ha' done a piece of work for which I am to be seised of seven farms in Kent land. See yo'—they send me messengers with money to Calais gate.' He pointed his thumb at the young Poins.

The boy, to prove that he was no common messenger, drew his right leg up and said:

'Nay, goodman Squire; an ye had slain the Cardinal the farms should have been yours. As it lies, ye are no more than lieutenant of Calais stone barges.'

'Thou liest,' Culpepper answered negligently, not turning his gaze from the gatewarden to whom he addressed a friendly question of, Who was the woman that had brought the two of them down.

'Now, Squahre!' the Lincolnshire man grinned delightedly; 'thu hast askëd me tü questions. Answer me one: Did *thee* lie upon her when thee put her name up in the township of Stamford?'

'Stamford in Lincolnshire was thy townplace?' Culpepper asked. 'But who was thy woman? I ha' had so many women and lied about so many more that I never had!'

The Lincolnshire man threw his leather cap to the keystone of the archway, caught it again and set it upon his thatch of hair, having the solemnity of one who performs his rituals.

'Goodly squahre that thee art!' he said; 'thou has harmed a many wenches in truth and in lies.'

Culpepper spied a down feather on his knee.

'Curse the mattress that I lay upon this night,' he said amiably.

He set his head back and blew the feather high into the air so that it floated out towards the tranquil and sunny pasture fields of France.

'Cub!' he said to Hal Poins, 'take this as a lesson of the death that lies about the pilgrim's path. For why am I not a pilgrim? I was sent to rid Paris of a Cardinal Pole, who, being in league with the devil, hath a magic tongue. Mark this story well, cub, who art sent me with money and gifts from the King in his glory to me that sit upon a stone. Now mark—' He extended his white hand. 'This hand, o' yestereen, had a ring with a great green stone. Now no ring is here. It was given me by my seventeenth leman, who had two eyes that looked not together. No twelve robbers had taken it from me by force, since I had made a pact with the devil that these wall eyes should never look across my face whilst that ring was there. Now, God knows, I may find her in Calais. So mark well——' He had been sent to Paris to rid France of the Cardinal Pole; for the Cardinal Pole, being a succubus of the fiend, had a magical tongue and had been inducing the French King to levy arms, in the name of that arch-devil, the Bishop of Rome, against their goodly King Henry, upon whom God shed His peace. Culpepper raised his bonnet at the Deity's name, stuck it far back on his red head, and continued: Therefore the mouth of Cardinal Pole was to be stayed in Paris town.

Culpepper smote his breast ferociously and with a black pride.

'And I have stayed it!' he peacocked. 'I and no other. I—T. Culpepper—a made man!'

'Not so,' Poins answered stubbornly. 'Thou wast sent to Paris to slay, and thou hast not slain!'

'Thou liest!' Culpepper asseverated. 'I was sent to purge Paris town, and I ha' purged un. No pothicary had done it better nor Hercules that was a stall groom and cleaned stables in antick days.' For, at the first breath of news that Culpepper was in the town, at the first rumour that the king's assassin was in Paris, Cardinal Pole had gathered his purple skirts about his knees; at the second sound he had cast them off altogether and, arrayed as a woman or a barber's leech, had fled hot foot to Brescia and thence to Rome.

'That was a nothing!' Culpepper asseverated. 'Though I ha' heard said that Hercules was made a god for cleaning stables that he found no easy task. But I will grant that it was no task for me to cleanse a whole town. For I needed no besoms, nor even no dagger, but the mere shadow of my beard upon the cobbly stones of Paris sufficed. I say nothing of that which befel in the day's journey; but mark this! mark what follows!' He had set out from Paris upon a high horse, with a high heart; he had frighted off all robbers and all sturdy rogues upon the road; he had slept at good inns as became a made man, and had bought himself a goodly pair of embroidered gloves which he could well pay for out of his superfluity. Being in haste to reach England, where he had that that called for him, he had ridden through the town of Ardres at nightfall, being minded to ride his horse dead, reach Calais gates in the hour, and beat down the gate if the warder would not suffer him to enter, it being dark. But outside the town of Ardres upon a make of no man's ground, being neither French nor English, he had espied a hut, and in the dark hut a lighted window hole that sparkled bravely, and, within, a big, fair woman drinking wine between candles with the light in her hair and a white tablecloth. And, feeling goodly, and Calais gate being shut, whether he broke it down one hour or three hours later was all one to him. He had gone into the hut to take by force or for payment a glass of wine from the black jacks, a kiss from the woman's mouth, and what else of ease the place afforded.

'Now I will have you mark, cub,' he said—'cub that shall have to learn many wiles if thy throat be not cut by me within the next two hours. Mark this, cub: these were no Egyptians!' They were not Bohemians, not swearers, not subtle cozeners, not even black a-vised, or he would have been on his guard against them; but they were plain, fair folks of Normandy. So he had drunk his wine, and cast a main or two at dice with the woman and two men, losing no more and no less than was decent. And he had drunk more wine and had taken his kisses—since it was all one whether he came three hours or four hours later to Calais gate. And there had been candles on the table and stuffs upon the wall, and a crock on the fire for mulling the wine, and a sheet upon the feather bed. But when he awoke in the morning he had lain upon the hard earth, between the bare walls. And all that was his was gone that was worth the taking.

'Now mark, cub,' he said. 'It was a simple thing this flitting with the hangings and the clothes and the pot rolled in bales and hung upon my horse. Upon my horse! But what is not simple is that simple folk of

Normandy should have learned the arts of subtlety and drugging of wines. Mark that!' He pointed a finger at Poins.

'Had God been good to you you might have been as good a warring boy as Thomas Culpepper, who with the shadow of his hand held back the galleons of France and France's knights from the goodly realm of England. For this I have done by frighting from Paris, Cardinal Pole that was moving the French King to war on us. Had God been good to you you might have been as brave. But marvel and consider and humble you in the dust to think that a man with my brain pan and all it holds could have been so cozened. For sure, a dolt like you would have been stripped more clean till you had neither nails to your toes nor hair to your eyebrows.'

Hal Poins snarled that Culpepper would have been shaved too but that red hair stunk in the nostrils even of cozeners and thieves.

Culpepper wagged his head from side to side.

'This is a main soft stone,' he said; 'I am main weary. When the stone grows hard, which is a sign that I shall no longer be minded to rest, I will break thy back with a cudgel.'

Poins stamped his foot with rage and tears filled his eyes.

'An thou had a sword!' he said. 'An only thou had a sword!'

'A year-old carrot to baste thee with!' Culpepper answered. 'Swords are for men!' He turned to Hogben, who was sitting on the ground furbishing his pikehead. 'Heard you the like of my tale?' he asked lazily.

'Oh aye!' the Lincolnshire man answered. 'The simple folk of Normandy are simple only because they have no suitors. But they ha' learned that marlock from the sailors of Rye town. For in Rye town, which is the sinkhole of Sussex, you will meet every morning ten travellers travelling to France in the livery of Father Adam. Normans can learn,' he added sententiously, 'as the beasts of the field can learn from a man. My father had a ewe lamb that danced a pavane to my pipe on the farm of Sallowford that you sold to buy a woman the third part of a gown.'

'Why! Art Nick Hogben?' Culpepper said.

'Hast that question answered,' Hogben said. 'Now answer me one. Liedst thou when saidst what thou saidst of that wurman?'

Culpepper on the stone swung his legs vaingloriously:

'I sold three farms to buy her a gown,' he said.

'Aye!' Nick Hogben answered. 'So thou saidst in Stamford town three years gone by. And thou saidst more and the manner of it. But betwixt the buying the gowns and the more of it lie many things. As this: Did she take the gown of thee? Or as this: Having taken the gown of thee, did she pay thee in the kind payment should be made in?'

Culpepper looked up at him with a sharp snarl.

'For—' and Nick Hogben shook his head sagaciously, 'Stamford town believed the more and the manner of it, and Kat Howard's name is up in the town of Stamford. But I have not yet chiselled out the great piece that shall come from my pike when certain sure I am that Kat Howard is down under a man's foot.'

Culpepper rose suddenly to his feet and wagged a finger at Hogben.

'Now I am minded to wed Kat Howard!' he said. 'Therefore I will say I lied then. But as for what you shall think, consider that I had her alone many days and nights; consider that though she be over learned in the Latin tongues that set a woman against joyment, I have a proper person and a strong wrist, a pleasant tongue but a hot and virulent purpose. Consider that she welly starved in her father, the Lord Edmund's, house and I had pies and gowns for her. Consider these things and make a hole or no hole as thou wilt——'

Nicholas Hogben considered with his eyes on the ground; he scratched his head with a black finger.

'I can make nowt out,' he said. 'But I will curse thee for a lily-livered hoggit an thou marry Kat Howard.'

'Why, I am minded to marry her,' Culpepper answered, 'over here in France,' and he stretched a hand towards the long white road where in the distance the French peasants were driving lean beasts for a true Englishman's provender in Calais. 'Over here in France. Body of God!— Body of God!——' He wavered, being still fevered. 'In England it had been otherwise. But here, shivering across plains and seas—why, I will wed with her.'

'Talkest like a Blind God Boy,' Hogben said sarcastically. 'How knowest she be thine to take?' He pointed at the young Poins. 'Here be another hath had doings with a Kat Howard, though I cannot well discern if she be thine or whose.'

Culpepper sprang, a flash of green, straight at the callow boy. But Poins had sprung too, back and to the left, and his oiled sword was from its scabbard and warring in the air.

'Holy Sepulchre! I will spit thee—Holy Sepulchre! I will spit thee!' he cried.

'Ass!' Culpepper answered. 'In God's time I will break thy back across my knee. But God's time is not yet.'

He poured out a flood of questions about the Kat Howard Poins had seen.

'Squahre Thomas,' Nicholas Hogben interrupted him maliciously, 'that young man of Kent saith e'ennow: "Kat Howard is like to——" and then he chokes upon his words. Now even what make of thing is it that Kat Howard is like to do or be done by?'

With his sword whiffling before him the young Poins could think rapidly— nay, upon any matter that concerned his advancement he could think rapidly always.

'Goodman Thomas Culpepper,' he said in a high voice, 'the mistress Katharine Howard I spoke of is thin and dark and small, and married to Edward Howard of Biggleswade. She is like to die of a quinsy.'

For well he knew that his advancement depended on his keeping Thomas Culpepper on the hither side of the water; and if it muddled his brain to have been so usefully mishandled for carrying letters betwixt the King's Grace and the Lady Katharine Howard, he knew enough of a jealous man to know that that was no news to keep Thomas Culpepper in Calais.

Culpepper's animation dropped like the light of a torch that is dowsed.

'Put up thy pot skewer,' he said; 'my Kat is tall and fairish and unwed. Ha' ye not seen her with the Lady Mary of England's women?'

The young Poins, zealous to be rid of the matter, answered fervently:

'Never. She is not talked of in the Court.'

'That is the best hearing,' Thomas Culpepper said. 'I do absolve thee of five kicks for being the messenger of that.'

III

They were a-walking in the little garden below the windows of the late Cardinal's house at Hampton; the April sun shone, for May came on apace, and in that sheltered spot the light lay warm and no breezes came. They took great pleasure there beneath the windows. One girl kept three golden balls flying in the air, whilst three others and two lords sought to distract her by inducing her little hound to bark shrilly below her hands up at the flying balls that caught in them the light of the sun, the blue of the sky, and the red and grey of the warm palace walls. Down the nut walk, where the trees that the dead Cardinal had set were already fifteen years old and dark with young green leaves as bright as little flowers, they had set up archery targets. Cicely Elliott, in black and white, flashing like a magpie in the alleys, ran races with the Earl of Surrey beneath the blinking eyes of her old knight; the Lady Mary, herself habited all in black, moved like a dark shadow upon a dial between the little beds upon paths of red brick between box hedges as high as your ankles. She spoke to none save once when she asked the name of a flower. But laughter went up, and it seemed as if, in this first day out of doors, all the Court opened its lungs to drink the new air; and they were making plans for May Day already.

They asked, too, a riddle: 'An a nutshell from Candlemas loved a merry bud in March, how should it come to pleasure and content?' and men who had the answer looked wise and shook their sides at guessing faces.

In a bower at the south end of the small garden Katharine Howard sat to play cat's-cradle with the old lady of Rochford. This foolish game and this foolish old woman, with her unceasing tales of the Queen Anne Boleyn— who had been her cousin—gave to Katharine a great feeling of ease. With her troubled eyes and weary expression, her occasional groans as the rheumatism gnawed at her joints, the old lady minded her of the mother she had so seldom seen. She had always been somewhere away, all through Katharine's young years, planning and helping her father to advancement that never came, and hopeless to control her wild children. Thus Katharine had come to love this poor old woman and consorted much with her, for she was utterly bewildered to control the Lady Mary's maids that were beneath her care.

Katharine held out her hands, parallel, as if she were praying, with the strand of blue wool and silver cord criss-cross and diagonal betwixt her fingers. The old lady bent above them, silent and puzzled, to get the key to the strings. Twice she protruded her gouty fingers, with swollen ends; and twice she drew them back to stroke her brows.

'I mind,' she said suddenly, 'that I played cat's-cradle with my cousin Anne, that was a sinful queen.' She bent again and puzzled about the strings. 'In those days I had a great skill, I mind. We revised it to the eleventh change many times before her death.' Again she leant forward and again back. 'I did come near my death, too,' she added.

Katharine's eyes had been gazing past her; suddenly she asked:

'Was Anne Boleyn loved after she grew to be Queen?'

The old woman's face took on a palsied and haunted look.

'God help you!' she said; 'do you ask that?' and she glanced round her furtively in an agony of apprehension. Something had drawn all the gay gowns and embroidered stomachers towards the higher terrace. They were all alone in the arbour.

'Why,' Katharine said, 'so many innocent creatures have been done to death since Cromwell came, that, though she was lewd before and a heretic all her days, I think doubts may be.'

The old lady pressed her hand upon her bosom where her heart beat.

'Madam Howard,' she said, 'for my life I know not the truth of the matter. There was much trickery; God knoweth the truth.'

Katharine mused for a moment above the cat's-cradle on her fingers. Near the joint at the end of the little one there was a small mole.

'Take you the fifth and third strings,' she said. 'The king string holds your wrist,' and whilst the old face was still intent upon the problem she said:

'I think that if a woman come to be Queen it is odds that she will live chastely, how lewd soever she ha' been aforetime.'

Lady Rochford set her fingers in between Katharine's, but when she drew them back with the strings upon them, they wavered, lost their straightness, knotted and then resolved themselves into a single loop as in a swift wind a cloud dies away beneath the eyes of the beholder.

'Why, 'tis pity,' Katharine said.

All the lords and all the ladies were now upon the terrace above. The old lady had the string in her broad lap. Suddenly she bent forward, her eyes opened.

'She was the enemy of your Church,' she said. 'But this I will tell you: upon occasions when men swore she had been with other men o' nights, the Queen was in my bed with me!'

Katharine nodded silently.

'Who was I that I dare speak?' the old woman sobbed; and Katharine nodded again.

Lady Rochford rubbed together her fat hands as she were ringing them.

'Before God,' she moaned, 'and by the blessed blood of Hailes that cured ever my pains, if a soul know a soul I knew Anne. If she was a woman like other women before she wedded the King, she was minded to be chaste after. Madam Howard,'—and she rocked her fat body to and fro upon the seat—'they came to me from both sides, your Papists and her heretics; they threatened me to keep silence of what I knew. I was to keep silence. I name no names. But they came o' both sides, Papists and heretics; though she was middling true to the heretics they could not be true to her.'

Katharine answered her own thoughts with:

'Ay; but my cause is the good cause. Men shall be true to it.'

The old lady leaned forward and stroked her hands.

'Dearie,' she said, 'dandling piece, sweet bit, there are no true men.' She had an entreaty in her tone, and her large blue eyes gazed fixedly. 'Say that my cousin Anne was a heretic. I know naught of it save that my bones have ached always since the holy blood of Hailes was done away with that was wont to cure me. But the Queen Anne was hard driven because of a plotting; and no man stood her friend.' With her large and tear-filled eyes she gazed at the palace, where the pear trees upon the walls shewed new, pale leaves in the sunlight. 'The great Cardinal was hard driven because of a plot, and no man was true to him. There is no true man. Hope not for one. Hope not for any one. The great Cardinal builded those walls and that palace—and where is he?'

'Yet,' Katharine said, 'Privy Seal that is was true to him and profited exceedingly.'

Lady Rochford shook her head.

'For a little while truth may help you,' she said; 'but your name in the end shall be but a stink.'

'Ay,' Katharine answered her; 'but ye shall gain at the end of all. For I hold it for certain that because, to the uttermost dregs of his cup, Cromwell was true to his master Wolsey, before the throne of God much shall be pardoned him.'

The old woman answered bitterly:

'The throne of God is a long way from here.'

'Please it Mary and the saints,' Katharine said, 'the ten years to come shall bring Heaven a thousand leagues nearer to this land.' But her words died away because the Lady Rochford's mouth fell open.

From the terrace a great square man led down a tiny, small man, giving the child his finger to help him down the steps. It clung to him, the little, squared replica of himself, sturdily and with a blonde, small face laughing up into his father's that laughed down past a huge shoulder. Henry was dressed all in black, and his son too; the boy's callow head shone in the sunshine, and they came dallying down the little path, many faces and shoulders peering over the terrace wall at them. Once the child stumbled, loosed his hold of his father's finger and came down upon all fours. He crawled to the pathside, filled his little hands with leaves, and held them up towards his sire; and they could hear the King say:

'Who-hoop, Ned! Princes walk not like quadrumanes,' as he bent to take the leaves. The child twisted himself, gripping his little fingers into Henry's garter, and, catching again at his finger, pulled his father towards their bower.

The Lady Rochford rose, but Katharine sat where she was to smile upon the child and brush his head with a pink tassel of her sleeve. The little prince hid his face in the voluminous velvet of his father's vast thighs. The King, diffusing a great and embracing pride, laughed to Lady Rochford.

'Ye played cat's-cradle,' he said. 'I warrant ye brought it not beyond seven changes. Time was when I have done fourteen with a lady if her hands were white enough.'

He threw away the green leaves of the clove pinks that his son had given him, and took the blue and silver loop from the old woman's hands. He sat himself heavily on the bench facing Katharine, and crying, 'See you, silly Ned,' held his son's hands apart and fitted the cord over the little wrists.

Suddenly he bent clumsily forward and picked up again the carnation leaves that lay in green strands upon the floor of the arbour, grunting a little with the effort.

'This is the first offering my son ever made me,' he said, and he drew a pocket purse from his breast to lay them in. 'Please God he shall yet lay at my feet a province or two of our heritage of France.' He touched his cap at the Deity's name, and called gruffly at his son: 'See you, forget not ever that we be Kings of France too, you and I,' and the little boy with his cropped head uttered:

'*Rex Angliae, Galliae, Franciae et Hiberniae!*'

'Aye, I ha' learned ye that,' the King said, and roared with laughter. Of a sudden he turned his head, without moving his body, towards Katharine.

'I ha' news from Norfolk in France,' he said, and, as the Lady Rochford made to move, he uttered good-naturedly: 'Aye, avoid. But ye may buss my son.'

He stretched back his head, laid an arm along the back of his seat, put out his feet and pushed at the child, who played with his shoe-tags.

'The boy grows,' he said, and motioned for Katharine to sit beside him. Then his face shewed a quick dissatisfaction. 'A brave boy, but a should be braver,' and looking down, 'see you not blue lines about 's gills?' He caught at her hand with a masterful grip.

'Here we're a picture,' he said: 'a lusty husbandman, his lusty son, his lusty wife, resting all beneath his goodly vine.' His face clouded again. 'I—I am not lusty; my son, he is not lusty.' He touched her cheek. 'Thou art lusty enow—hast such pink cheeks.'

'Aye, we were always lusty at home when we had enow to eat,' Katharine said. She took the child upon her knee and blew lightly in his face. 'I will wager you I will guess his weight within a pound,' she added, and began to play a game with the tiny fingers. 'Wherefore do ye habit little children in black?'

'Why,' the King answered, 'I know not if I myself appear less monstrous in black or red, and my son shall be habited as I be. 'Tis to make the trial.'

'Aye,' Katharine said, 'ye think first of yourself. But dress the child in white and go in white yourself. And set up a chantry of priests to pray the child grow sturdy. It was thus my cousin Surrey's life was saved that was erst a weakling.'

'Be Queen,' he said suddenly. 'Marry me. I came here to ask it.'

Her lips parted; she left her hand in his. The expected words had come.

'I have thought on it,' she said. 'I knew ye could not long hold to child and sire as ye sware ye would.'

'Kat,' he said, 'ye shall do my will. I ha' news from France. Ye gave me good rede. I ha' news from Cleves: the Cleves woman shall no more be queen of mine. Thee I will have.'

She raised herself from the bench and turned in the entrance of the arbour to look at him.

'Give me leave to walk on the path,' she said. 'I have thought on this—for I was sure I gave you good advice, and well I knew Cleves would sever from ye.' She faltered: 'I ha' thought on it. But 'tis different to think on it and to ha' the thing in your face.'

He uttered, 'Make haste,' and she walked down the path. He saw her, tall, fair, swaying a little in the wind, raise her face to the skies; her long fingers made the sign of the cross, her hood fell back. Her lips moved; the fringes of her lashes came down over her blue eyes, and she seemed to wrestle with her hands.

'Aye,' he muttered to himself half earnest, half sardonic, 'prayer is better than thoughts. God strike with palsy them that made me afraid to pray.... Aye, pray on, pray on,' he said again. 'But by God and His wounds! ye shall be my queen.'

By the time she came back he laughed at her tempestuously, and pushing the little prince tenderly with his huge foot, watched him roll on the floor catching at the air.

'Why,' he said to her, 'what's the whimsy now? Shalt be the queen. 'Tis the sole way. 'Tis the way to the light.' He leant forward. 'Cleves has gone to the bastard called Charles to sue for mercy. Ye led me so well to set Francis against Charles that I may snap my fingers against both. None but thee could ha' forged that bolt. Child, I will make a league with the Pope against Charles or Francis, with Francis or Charles. Anne may go hang herself.' He rose to his feet and stretched out both his hands, his eyes glowing beneath his deep brows. 'Body o' God! thou art a very fair woman; and now I will be such a king as never was, and take France for mine own and set up Holy Church again, and say good prayers and sleep in a warm bed. Body o' God! Body o' God!'

'God and the saints save the issue!' she said. 'I am thy servant and slave.'

But her tone made him recoil.

'What whimsy's here?' he muttered heavily, and his eyes became suffused with red. 'Speak, wench!' He pulled at the stuff round his throat. 'I will have peace,' he said. 'I will at last have peace.'

'God send you have it,' she said, and trembled a little, half in fear, half in sheer pity at the thought of thwarting him.

'Speak thy fool whimsy,' he muttered huskily. 'Speak!'

'My lord,' she said, 'where is the Queen that is?'

He flared suddenly at her as if she had reproved him.

'At Windsor. 'Tis a better palace than this of mine here.' He shook his finger heavily and uttered with a boastful defiance: 'Shalt not say I shower no gifts on her. Shalt not say she has no state. I ha' sent her seven jennets this day. I shall go bring her golden apples on the morrow. Scents she has had o' me; French gowns, Southern fruits. No man nor wench shall say I be not princely——' His boasting bluster died away before her silence. To please a mute desire in her, he had showered more gifts on Anne of Cleves than on any other woman he had ever seen; and thinking that she used him ill not to praise him for this, he could not hold his tongue: 'What is't to thee what she hath? What she hath thou losest. 'Tis a folly.'

'My lord,' she said, 'I will myself to see the Queen that is.'

'And whysomever?' he voiced his astonishment.

'My lord,' she said, 'I have a tickly conscience in divorces. I will ask her mine own self.'

He roared out suddenly indistinguishable words, stamped his feet, waved his hands at the skies, and lost his voice altogether.

'Aye,' she said, catching at some of his speech, 'I ha' read your Highness' depositions. I ha' read depositions of the Archbishop's. But I will be satisfied of her own mouth that she be not your wife.'

And when he swore that Anne would lie:

'Nay,' she answered; 'if she will lie to keep her queenship, keep it she shall. I am upon the point of honour.'

'Before God!'—and his voice had a sneering haughtiness—'ye will not be long of this world if ye steer by the point of honour.'

'Sir,' she cried out and stretched forth her hands; 'for the love of Mary who guides the starry counsels and of the saints who sit in conclave, speak not in that wise.'

He shrugged his shoulders and said, with a touch of angry shame:

'God send the world were another world; I would it were other. But I am a prince in this one.'

'My lord,' she said; 'if the world so is, kings and princes are here to be above the world. In your greatness ye shall change it; with your justice ye shall purify it; with your clemencies ye should it chasten and amerce. Ye ask me to be a queen. Shall I be a queen and not such a queen? No, I tell you; if a woman may swear a great oath, I swear by Leonidas that saved Sparta and by Christ Jesus that saved this world, so will I come by my queenship and so act in it that, if God give me strength the whole world never shall find speck upon mine honour—or upon thine if I may sway thee.'

'Why,' he said, 'thy voice is like little flutes.'

He considered, patting his square, soft-shod feet upon the bricks of the arbour floor.

'By Guy! I will have thee,' he said; 'though ye twist my senses as never woman twisted them—and it is not good for a man to be swayed by his women.'

'My lord,' she said, 'in naught would I sway a man save in where my conscience pricks and impels me.' She rubbed her hand across her eyes. 'It is difficult to see the right in these matters. The only way is to be firm for God and for the cause of the saints.' She looked down at her feet. 'I will be ceaseless in my entreaties to you for them,' she uttered. Suddenly again she stretched forth both her hands that had sunk to her sides:

'Dear lord,' and her voice was full of pity for herself and for entreaty; 'let me go to a convent to pray unceasing for thee.'

He shook his head.

'Dear lord,' she repeated; 'use me as thou wilt and I will stay beside thee and urge thee to the cause of God.'

Again he shook his head.

'The saints would pardon me it,' she whispered; 'or if I even be damned to save England, it were a good burnt-offering.'

'Wench,' he said; 'I was never a man to go a-whoring. I ha' done it, but had no savour with it.' His boastfulness returned to the heavy voice. 'I am a king that will give. I will give a crown, a realm, jewels, honours, monies. All I have I will give; but thou shalt wed me.' He threw out his chest and gazed down at her. 'I was ever thus,' he said.

'And I ever thus,' she answered him swiftly. 'Mary hath put this thing in my mind; and though ye scourge me, ye shall not have it otherwise.'

'Even how?' he said.

'My lord,' she answered; 'if the Queen, so it be true, will say she be no wife of thine, I will wed thee. If the Queen, seeing that it is for the good of this suffering realm, will give to me her crown, I will wed with thee. I wot ye may get for yourself another woman with another gear of conscience to bear t'ee children. All the ills of this realm came with a divorce of a queen. I do hate the word as I hate Judas, and will have no truck with the deed.'

'Ye speak me hard,' he said; 'but no man shall say I could not bear with the truth at odd moments.'

A great and hasty eagerness came into her voice.

'Ye say that it is truth?' she cried. 'God hath softened thy heart.'

'God or thee,' he said, and muttered, 'I do not make this avowal to the world.' Suddenly he smote his thigh. 'Body o' God!' he called out; 'the day shall soon come. Cleves falls away, France and Spain are sundering. I will sue for peace with the Pope, and set up a chapel to Kat's memory.' He breathed as if a weight had fallen from his chest, and suddenly laughed: 'But ye must wed me to keep me in the right way.'

He changed his tone again.

'Why, go to Anne,' he said; 'she is such a fool she will not lie to thee; and, before God, she is no wife of mine.'

'God send ye speak the truth,' she answered; 'but I think few men be found that will speak truth in these matters.'

IV

But it was with Throckmorton that the real pull of the rope came. Henry was by then so full of love for her that, save when she crossed his purpose, he would have given her her way to the bitter end of things. But Throckmorton bewailed her lack of loyalty. He came to her on the morning of the next day, having heard that, if the rain held off, a cavalcade of seventeen lords, twelve ladies and their bodyguards were commanded to ride with her in one train to Windsor, where the Queen was.

'I am main sure 'tis for Madam Howard that this cavalcade is ordered,' he said; 'for there is none other person in Court to whom his Highness would work this honour. And I am main sure that if Madam Howard goeth, she goeth with some mad maggot of a purpose.'

His foxy, laughing eyes surveyed her, and he stroked his great beard deliberately.

'I ha' not been near ye this two month,' he said, 'but God knows that I ha' worked for ye.'

Save to take her to Privy Seal the day before, when Privy Seal had sent him, he had in truth not spoken with her for many weeks. He had deemed it wise to keep from her.

'Nevertheless,' he said earnestly, 'I know well that thy cause is my cause, and that thou wilt spread upon me the mantle of thy favour and protection.'

They were in her old room with the green hangings, the high fireplace, and before the door the red curtain worked with gold that the King had sent her, and Cromwell had given orders that the spy outside should be removed, for he was useless. Thus Throckmorton could speak with a measure of freedom.

'Madam Howard,' he said; 'ye use me not well in this. Ye are not so stable nor so safe in your place as that ye may, without counsel or guidance, risk all our necks with these mad pranks.'

'Goodman,' she said, 'I asked ye not to come into my barque. If ye hang to the gunwale, is it my fault an ye be drowned in my foundering if I founder?'

'Tell me why ye go to Windsor,' he urged.

'Goodman,' she answered, 'to ask the Queen if she be the King's wife.'

'Oh, folly!' he cried out, and added softly, 'Madam Howard, ye be monstrous fair. I do think ye be the fairest woman in the world. I cannot sleep for thinking on thee.'

'Poor soul!' she mocked him.

'But, bethink you,' he said; 'the Queen is a woman, not a man. All your fairness shall not help you with her. Neither yet your sweet tongue nor your specious reasons. Nor yet your faith, for she is half a Protestant.'

'If she be the King's wife,' Katharine said, 'I will not be Queen. If she care enow for her queenship to lie over it, I will not be Queen either. For I will not be in any quarrel where lies are—either of my side or of another's.'

'God help us all!' Throckmorton mocked her. 'Here is my neck engaged on your quarrel—and by now a dozen others. Udal hath lied for you in the Cleves matter; so have I. If ye be not Queen to save us ere Cromwell's teeth be drawn, our days are over and past.'

He spoke with so much earnestness that Katharine was moved to consider her speaking.

'Knight,' she said at last, 'I never asked ye to lie to Cromwell over the Cleves matter. I never asked Udal. God knows, I had the rather be dead than ye had done it. I flush and grow hot each time I think this was done for me. I never asked ye to be of my quarrel—nay, I take shame that I have not ere this sent to Privy Seal to say that ye have lied, and Cleves is false to him.' She pointed an accusing finger at him: 'I take shame; ye have shamed me.'

He laughed a little, but he bent a leg to her.

'Some man must save thee from thy folly's fruits,' he said. 'For some men love thee. And I love thee so my head aches.'

She smiled upon him faintly.

'For that, I believe, I have saved thy neck,' she said. 'My conscience cried: "Tell Privy Seal the truth"; my heart uttered: "Hast few men that love thee and do not pursue thee."'

Suddenly he knelt at her feet and clutched at her hand.

'Leave all this,' he said. 'Ye know not how dangerous a place this is.' He began to whisper softly and passionately. 'Come away from here. Well ye know that I love 'ee better than any man in land. Well ye know. Well ye know. And well ye know no man could so well fend for ye or jump nimbly to thy thoughts. The men here be boars and bulls. Leave all these dangers;

here is a straight issue. Ye shall not sway the wild boar king for ever. Come with me.'

As she did not at once find words to stop his speech, he whispered on:

'I have gold enow to buy me a baron's fee in Almain. I have been there: in castles in the thick woods, silken bowers may be built——'

But suddenly again he rose to his feet and laughed:

'Why,' he said, 'I hunger for thee: at times 'tis a madness. But 'tis past.'

His eyes twinkled again and he waved a hand.

'Mayhap 'tis well that ye go to the Queen,' he said drily. 'If the Queen say, "Yea," ye ha' gained all; if "Nay" ye ha' lost naught, for ye may alway change your mind. And a true and steadfast cause, a large and godly innocence is a thing that gaineth men's hearts and voices.' He paused for a moment. 'Ye ha' need o' man's good words,' he said drily; then he laughed again. 'Aye: *Nolo episcopari* was always a good cry,' he said.

Katharine looked at him tenderly.

'Ye know my aims are other,' she said, 'or else you would not love me. I think ye love me better than any man ever did—though I ha' had a store of lovers.'

'Aye,' he nodded at her gravely, 'it is pleasant to be loved.'

She was sitting by her table and leant her hand upon her cheek; she had been sewing a white band with pearls and silken roses in red and leaves in green, and it fell now to her feet from her lap. Suddenly he said:

'Answer me one question of three?'

She did not move, for a feeling of languor that often overcame her in Throckmorton's presence made her feel lazy and apt to listen. She itched to be Queen—on the morrow or next day; she desired to have the King for her own, to wear fair gowns and a crown; to be beloved of the poor people and beloved of the saints. But her fate lay upon the knees of the gods then: on the morrow the Queen would speak—betwixt then and now there was naught for it but to rest. And to hearken to Throckmorton was to be surprised as if she listened at a comedy.

'One question of three may be answered,' she said.

'On the forfeit of a kiss,' he added. 'I pray God ye answer none.'

He pondered for a moment, and leaning back against the chimney-piece crossed one silk-stockinged, thin, red leg. He spoke very swiftly, so that his words were like lightning.

'And the first is: An ye had never come here but elsewhere seen me, had ye it in you to ha' loved me? And the second: How ye love the King's person? And the third: Were ye your cousin's leman?'

Leaning against the table she seemed slowly to grow stiff in her pose; her eyes dilated; the colour left her cheeks. She spoke no word.

'Privy Seal hath sent a man to hasten thy cousin back to here,' he said at last, after his eyes had steadily surveyed her face. She sat back in her chair, and the strip of sewing fell to wreathe, white and red and green, round her skirts on the floor.

'I have sent a botcher to stay his coming,' he said slowly. 'Thy maid Margot's brother.'

'I had forgotten Tom,' she said with long pauses between her words. She had forgotten her cousin and playmate. She had given no single thought to him since a day that she no longer remembered.

Reading the expression of her face and interpreting her slow words, Throckmorton was satisfied in his mind that she had been her cousin's.

'He hath passed from Calais to Dover, but I swear to you that he shall never come to you,' he said. 'I have others here.' He had none, but he was set to comfort her.

'Poor Tom!' she uttered again almost in a whisper.

'Thus,' he uttered slowly, 'you have a great danger.'

She was silent, thinking of her Lincolnshire past, and he began again:

'Therefore ye have need of help from me as I from thee.'

'Aye,' he said, 'you shall advise with me. For at least, if I may not have the pleasure of thy body, I will have the enjoyment of thy converse.' His voice became husky for a moment. 'Mayhap it is a madness in me to cling to thee; I do set in jeopardy my earthly riches and my hope of profit. But it is Macchiavelli who says: "*If ye hoard gold and at the end have not pleasure in what gold may pay, ye had better have loitered in pleasing meadows and hearkened to the madrigals of sweet singing fowls.*"' He waved his hand: 'Ye see I be still somewhat of a philosopher, though at times madness takes me.'

She was still silent—shaken into thinking of the past she had had with her cousin when she had been very poor in Lincolnshire; she had had leisure to read good letters there, and the time to think of them. Now she had not held a book for four days on end.

'You are in a very great danger of your cousin,' Throckmorton was repeating. 'Yet I will stay his coming.'

'Knight,' she said, 'this is a folly. If guards be needed to keep me from his knife, the King shall give me guards.'

'His knife!' Throckmorton raised his hands in mock surprise. 'His knife is a very little thing.'

'Ye would not say it an ye had come anear him when he was crossed,' she said. 'I, who am passing brave, fear his knife more than aught else in this world.'

'Oh, incorrigible woman,' he cried, 'thinking ever of straight things and clear doings. It is not the knife of your cousin, but the devious policy of Privy Seal that calleth for fear.'

'Why, or ever Privy Seal bind Tom to his policy he shall bind iron bars to make a coil.'

He looked at her with lifted eyebrows, and then scratched with his finger nail a tiny speck of mud from his shoe-point, balancing himself back against the chimney piece and crossing his red legs above the knees.

'Madam Howard,' he said, 'Privy Seal is minded to use thy cousin for a battering-ram.' She was hardly minded to listen to him, and he uttered stealthily, as if he were sure of moving her: 'Thy cousin shall breach a way to the ears of the King—for thy ill fame to enter in.'

She leaned forward a little.

'Tell me of my ill fame,' she said; and at that moment Margot Poins, her handmaid, placid still, large, fair and florid, came in to bring her mistress an embroidery frame of oak wood painted with red stripes. At Throckmorton's glance askance at the cow-like girl, Katharine said: 'Ye may speak afore Margot Poins. I ha' heard tales of her bringing.'

Margot kneeled at Katharine's feet to stretch a white linen cloth over the frame on the floor.

'Privy Seal planneth thus,' Throckmorton answered Katharine's challenge. He spoke low and level, hoping to see her twinge at every new phrase. 'The King hath put from him every tale of thee; it is not easy to bring him tales of those he loves, but very dangerous. But Cromwell planneth to bring hither thy cousin and to keep him privily till one day cometh the King to be alone with thee in thy bower or his. Then, having removed all lets, shall Cromwell gird this cousin to spring in upon thee and the King, screaming out and with his sword drawn.' Still Katharine did not move, but leaned along her table of yellow wood. 'It is not the sword ye shall fear,' he said slowly, 'but what cometh after. For, for sure, Privy Seal holdeth, then shall be the time to bring witnesses against thee to the hearing of the King. And Privy Seal hath witnesses.'

'He would have witnesses,' Katharine answered.

'There be those that will swear——'

'Aye,' she caught him up, speaking very calmly. 'There be those that will swear they ha' seen me with a dozen men. With my cousin, with Nick Ardham, with one and another of the hinds. Why, he will bring a hind to swear I ha' loved him. And he will bring a bastard child or twain——' She paused, and he paused too.

At last he said: 'Anan?'

'Ye might do it against Godiva of Coventry, against the blessed Katharine or against Caesar's helpmeet in those days,' Katharine said. 'Margot here can match all thy witnesses from the city of London—men that never were in Lincolnshire.'

Margot's face flushed with a tide of exasperation, and, sitting motionless, she uttered deeply:

'My uncle the printer hath a man will swear he saw ye walk with a fiend having horns and a tail.' And indeed these things were believed among the Lutherans that flocked still to Margot's uncle's printing room. 'My uncle hath printed this,' she muttered, and fumbled hotly in her bosom. She drew out a sheet with coarse black letters upon it and cast it across the floor with a flushed disdain at Throckmorton's feet. It bore the heading: '*Newes from Lincoln*,' Throckmorton kicked with his toe the white scroll and scrutinised Katharine's face dispassionately with his foxy eyes that jumped between his lids like little beetles of blue. He thrust his cap back upon his head and laughed.

'Before God!' he said; 'ye are the joyfullest play that ever I heard. And how will Madam Howard act when the King heareth these things?'

Katharine opened her lips with surprise.

'For a subtile man ye are strangely blinded,' she said; 'there is one plain way.'

'To deny it and call the saints to witness!' he laughed.

'Even that,' she answered. 'I pray the saints to give me the place and time.'

'Ha' ye seen the King in a jealous rage?' he asked.

'Subtile man,' she answered, 'the King knows his world.'

'Aye,' he answered, 'knoweth that women be never chaste.'

Katharine bent to pick up her sewing.

'Sir,' she said, 'if the King will not have faith in me I will wed no King.'

His jaw fell. 'Ye have so much madness?' he asked.

She stretched towards him the hand that held her sewing now.

'I swear to you,' she said—'and ye know me well—I seek a way to bring these rumours to the King's ears.'

He said nothing, revolving these things in his mind.

'Goodly servant,' she began, and he knew from the round and silvery sound she drew from her throat that she was minded to make one of the long speeches that appalled and delighted him with their childish logic and wild honour. 'If it were not that my cousin would run his head into danger I would will that he came to the King. Sir, ye are a wise man, can ye not see this wisdom? There is no good walking but upon sure ground, and I will not walk where the walking is not good. Shall I wed this King and have these lies to fear all my life? Shall I wed this King and do him this wrong? Neither wisdom nor honour counsel me to it. Since I have heard these lies were abroad I have at frequent moments thought how I shall bring them before the King.'

He thrust his hands into his pockets, stretched his legs out, and leaned back as though he were supporting the chimney-piece with his back.

'The King knoweth how men will lie about a woman,' she began again. 'The King knoweth how ye may buy false witness as ye may buy herrings in the market-place at so much a score. An the King were such a man as not to know these things, I would not wed with him. An the King were such a man as not to trust in me, I would not wed with him. I could have no peace. I could have no rest. I am not one that ask little, but much.'

'Why, you ask much of them that do support your cause,' he laughed from his private thinking.

'I do ask this oath of you,' she answered: 'that neither with sword nor stiletto, nor with provoked quarrel, nor staves, nor clubs, nor assassins, ye do seek to stay my cousin's coming.'

He cut across her purpose with asking again: 'Ha' ye seen the King rage jealously?'

'Knight,' she said, 'I will have your oath.' And, as he paused in thought, she said: 'Before God! if ye swear it not, I will make the King to send for him hither guarded and set around with an hundred men.'

'Ye will not have him harmed?' he asked craftily. 'Ye do love him better than another?'

She rose to her feet, her lips parted. 'Swear!' she cried.

His fingers felt around his waist, then he raised his hand and uttered:

'I do swear that ne with sword ne stiletto, ne with staves nor with clubs, ne with any quarrels nor violence so never will I seek thy goodly cousin's life.'

He shook his head slowly at her.

'All the men ye have known have prayed ye to be rid of him,' he said; 'ye will live to rue.'

'Sir,' she answered him, 'I had rather live to rue the injury my cousin should do me than live to rue the having injured him.' She paused to think for a moment. 'When I am Queen,' she said, 'I will have the King set him in a command of ships to sail westward over the seas. He shall have the seeking for the Hesperides or the city of Atalanta, where still the golden age remains to be a model and ensample for us.' Her eyes looked past Throckmorton. 'My cousin hath a steadfast nature to be gone on such pilgrimages. And I would the discovery were made, this King being King and I his Queen; rather that than the regaining of France; more good should come to Christendom.'

'Madam Howard,' Throckmorton grinned at her, 'if men of our day and kin do come upon any city where yet remaineth the golden age, very soon shall be shewn the miracle of the corruptibility of gold. The rod of our corruption no golden state shall defy.'

She smiled friendlily at him.

'There we part company,' she said. 'For I do believe God made this world to be bettered. I think, and answer your question, I could never ha' loved you. For you be a child of the new Italians and I a disciple of the older holders of that land, who wrote, Cato voicing it for them, "Virtue spreadeth even as leaven leaveneth bread; a little lump in your flour in the end shall redeem all the loaf of the Republic."'

He smiled for a moment noiselessly, his mouth open but no sound coming out. Then he coaxed her:

'Answer my two other questions.'

'Knight,' she answered; 'for the truth of the last, ask, with thumbscrews, the witnesses ye found in Lincolnshire, and believe them as ye list. Or ask at the mouth of a draw-well if fishes be below in the water before ye ask a woman if she be chaste. For the other, consider of my actions hereafter if I do love the King's person.'

'Why, then, I shall never have kiss from mouth of thine,' he said, and pulled his cap down over his eyes to depart.

'When the sun shall set in the east,' she retorted, and gave him her hand to kiss.

Margot Poins raised her large, fair head from her stitching after he was gone, and asked:

'Tell me truly how ye love the King's person. Often I ha' thought of it; for I could love only a man more thin.'

'Child,' Katharine answered, 'his Highness distilleth from his person a make of majesty; there is no other such a man in Christendom. His Highness culleth from one's heart a make of pity—for, for sure, there is not in Christendom a man more tried or more calling to be led Godwards. The Greek writers had a myth, that the two wings of Love were made of Awe and Pity. Flaws I may find in him; but hot anger rises in my heart if I hear him miscalled. I will not perjure myself at his bidding; but being with him, I will kneel to him unbidden. I will not, to be his queen, have word in a divorce, for I have no truck with divorces; but I will humble myself to his Queen that is to pray her give me ease and him if the marriage be not consummated. For, so I love him that I will humble mine own self in the dust; but so I love love and its nobleness that, though I must live and die a cookmaid, I will not stoop in evil ways.'

'There is no man worth that guise of love,' Margot answered, her voice coming gruff and heavy, 'not the magister himself. I ha' smote one kitchenmaid i' the face this noon for making eyes at him.'

V

'My mad nephew,' Master Printer Badge said to Throckmorton, 'shall travel down from his chamber anon. When ye shall see the pickle he is in ye shall understand wherefore it needeth ten minutes to his downcoming.' To Throckmorton's query he shook his dark, bearded head and muttered: 'Nay; ye used him for your own purposes. Ye should know better than I what is like to have befallen him.'

Throckmorton swallowed his haste and leant back against the edge of a press that was not at work. Of these presses there were four there in the middle of the room: tall, black, compounded of iron and wood, the square inwards of each rose and fell rhythmically above the flutter of the printed leaves that the journeymen withdrew as they rose, and replaced, white, unsullied and damp as they came together again. Along the walls the apprentice setters stood before the black formes and with abstruse, deliberate or hesitating expressions, made swift snatches at the little leaden dice. The sifting sound of the leads going home and the creak of the presses with the heavy wheeze of one printer, huge and grizzled like a walrus, pulling the press-lever back and bending forward to run his eyes across the type—wheeze, creak and click—made a level and monotonous sound.

'Ye drill well your men,' Throckmorton said lazily, and smoothed his white fingers, holding them up against the light, as if they of all things most concerned him.

He had received that day at Hampton a letter from the printer here in Austin Friars, sent hastening by the hands of the pressman whose idle machine he now leant against. 'Sir,' the letter said, 'my nephew saith urgently that T.C. is landed at Greenwich. He might not stay him. What this importeth best is yknown to your worshipful self. By the swaying of the sea which late he overpassed, being tempestive, and by other things, my nephew is rendered incoherent. That God may save you and guide your counsels and those of your master to the more advantaging of the Protestant religion that now, praised be God! standeth higher in the realm than ever it did, is the prayer of Jno. Badge the Younger.'

Throckmorton had hastened there to the hedges of Austin Friars at the fastest of his bargemen's oars. The printer had told him that, but that the business was the Lord Privy Seal's and, as he understood, went to the advantaging of Protestantism and the casting down of Popery, never would he ha' sent with the letter his own printer journeyman, busied as they were with printing of his great Bible in English.

'Here is an idle press,' he said, pointing at the mute and lugubrious instrument of black, 'and I doubt I ha' done wrong.' His moody brow beneath the black, dishevelled hair became overcast so that it wrinkled into great furrows like crowns. 'I doubt whether I have done wrong,' and he folded his immense bare arms, on which the hair was like a black boar's, and pondered. 'If I thought I had done wrong, I might not sleep seven nights.'

A printer yawned at his loom, and the great dark man shouted at him:

'Foul knave, ye show indolence! Wot ye that ye be printing the Word of God to send abroad in this land? Wot ye that for this ye shall stand with the elect in Heaven?' He turned upon Throckmorton. 'Sir,' he said, 'your master Cromwell advanceth the cause, therefore I ha' served him in this matter of the letter. But, sir, I am doubtful that, by losing one moment from the printing of the pure Word of God, I have not lost more time than a year's work of thy master.'

Throckmorton rubbed gently the long hand that he still held against the light.

'Ye fall away from Privy Seal?' he asked.

The printer gazed at him with glowering and suffused eyes, choking in his throat. He raised an enormous hand before Throckmorton's face.

'Courtier,' he cried, 'with this hand I ha' stopped an ox, smiting it between the eyes. Wo befal the man, traitor to Privy Seal, that I do meet and betwixt whose eyes this hand doth fall.' The hand quivered in the air with fury. 'I can raise a thousand 'prentices and a thousand journeymen to save Privy Seal from any peril; I can raise ten thousand citizens, and ten thousand to-morrow again from the shires by pamphlets of my printing; I can raise a mighty army thus to shield him from Papists and the devil's foul contrivances. An I were a Papist, I would pray to him, were he dead, as he were a saint.' Throckmorton moved his face a line or two backwards from the gesticulating ham of a hand, and blinked his eyes. 'My gold were Privy Seal's an he needed it; my blood were his and my prayers. Nevertheless,' and his voice took a more exalted note, 'one letter of the Word of God, God aiding it, is of more avail than Privy Seal, or I, and all those I can love, or he. With his laws and his nose for treason he hath smitten the Amalekites above the belt; but a letter of the Word of God can smite them hip and thigh, God helping.' He seemed again to choke in his throat, and said more quietly: 'But ye shall not think a man in land better loveth this godly flail of the monks.'

'Why, I do think ye would stand up against the King's self,' Throckmorton said, 'and I am glad to hear it.'

'Against all printers and temporal powers,' the printer answered. Amongst the apprentices and journeymen a murmur arose of acclamation or of denial, some being of opinion that the King was divine in origin and inspiration, but for the most part they supported their master, and Throckmorton's blue eyes travelled from one to the other.

But the printer heaved a sigh of satisfaction.

'God be thanked,' he said, 'that keepeth the hearts of princes and guideth with His breath all temporal occurrences.' Throckmorton was about to touch his cap at the name of Omnipotence, but remembering that he was among Protestants changed the direction of his hand and scratched his cheek among the little hairs of his beard; 'the signs are favourable that our good King's Highness shall still incline to our cause and Privy Seal's.'

Throckmorton said: 'Anan?'

'Aye,' the printer said heavily, 'good news is come of Cleves.'

'Ye ha' news from Cleves?' Throckmorton asked swiftly.

'From Cleves not,' the printer answered; 'but from the Court by way of Paris and thence from Cleves.' And to the interested spy he related, accurately enough, that a make of mouthing, mowing, magister of the Latin tongues had come from Paris, having stolen copies of the Cleves envoy's letters in that town, and that these letters said that Cleves was fast inclined to the true Schmalkaldner league of Lutherans and would pay tribute truly, but no more than that do fealty to the accursed leaguer of the Pope called Charles the Emperor.

Throckmorton inclined his cap at an angle to the floor.

'How had ye that news that was so secret?' he asked.

The printer shook his dark beard with an air of heavy pleasure.

'Ye have a great organisation of spies,' he said, 'but better is the whisper of God among the faithful.'

'Why,' Throckmorton answered, 'the magister Udal hath to his sweetheart thy niece Margot Poins.'

At her name the printer's eyes filled with a sudden and violent heat.

'Seek another channel,' he cried, and waved his arms at the low ceiling. 'Before the face of Almighty God I swear that I ha' no truck with Margot my niece. Since she has been sib with the whore of the devil called Kat

Howard, never hath she told me a secret through her paramour or elsewise. A shut head the heavy logget keepeth—let her not come within reach of my hand.' He swayed back upon his feet. 'Let her not come,' he said. He bent his brows upon Throckmorton. 'I marvel,' he uttered, 'that ye who are so faithful a servant o' Privy Seal's can have truck with the brother of my niece Margot.'

'Printer,' Throckmorton answered him, 'ye know well that when the leaven of Protestantism hath entered in there, houses are divided against themselves. A wench may be a foul Papist and serve, if ye will, Kat Howard; but her brother shall yet be an indifferent good servant for me.'

The printer, who had tolerated that his men should hear his panegyric of the Bible and Privy Seal, scowled at them now so that again the arms swung to and fro with the levers, the leads clicked. He put his great head nearer Throckmorton's and muttered:

'Are ye certain my nephew serveth ye well? He was never wont to favour our cause, and, before ye sent him on this errand, he was wont to cry out in his cups that he was disgraced for having carried letters betwixt Kat Howard and the King. If this were true he was no friend of ours.'

'Why, it was true,' Throckmorton uttered negligently.

The printer caught at the spy's wrist, and the measure of his earnestness showed the extent of his passion for Privy Seal's cause.

'Use him no more,' he said. 'Both children of my sister were ever indifferents. They shall not serve thee well.'

'It was ever Privy Seal's motto and habit to use for his servitors those that had their necks in his noose. Such men serve him ever the best.'

The printer shook his head gloomily.

'I wager my nephew will yet play the traitor to Privy Seal.'

'I will do it myself ere that,' and Throckmorton yawned, throwing his head back.

'The scaldhead is there,' the printer said; and in the doorway there stood, supporting himself by the lintel, the young Poins. His face was greenish white; a plaster was upon his shaven head; he held up one foot as if it pained him to set it to the floor. Through the house-place where sat the aged grandfather with his cap pulled over his brows, pallid, ironical and seeming indescribably ancient, the printer led the spy. The boy hobbled after them, neglecting the old man's words:

'Ha' no truck with men of Privy Seal's. Privy Seal hath stolen my ground.' In the long shed where they ate all, printer, grandfather, apprentices and journeymen, the printer thrust open the door with a heavy gesture, entering first and surveying the long trestles.

'Ye can speak here,' he said, and motioned away an aged woman. She bent above a sea coal fire on the hearth where boiled, hung from a hook, a great pot. The old thing, in short petticoats and a linsey woolsey bodice that had been purple and green, protested shrilly. Her crock was on the boil; she was not there to be driven away; she had work like other folk, and had been with the printer's mother eight years before he was born. His voice, raised to its height, was useless to drown her words. She could not hear him; and shrugging his shoulders, he said to Throckmorton that she heard less than the walls, and that was the best place he had for them to talk in. He slammed the door behind him.

Throckmorton set his foot upon the bench that ran between table and wall. He scowled fell-ly at the boy, so that his brows came down below his nose-top. 'Ye ha' not stayed him,' he said.

The boy burst forth in a torrent of rage and despair. He cursed Throckmorton to his face for having sent him upon this errand.

'I ha' been beaten by a gatewarden! by a knave! by a ploughman's son from Lincolnshire!' he cried. 'A' cracked my skull with a pikestave and kicked me about the ribs when I lay on the ship's floor, sick like a pig. God curse the day you sent me to Calais, a gentleman's son, to be beat by a boor!' He broke off and began again. 'God curse you and the day I saw you! God curse Kat Howard and the day I carried her letter! God curse my sister Margot and the day she gar'd me carry the letters! And may a swift death of the pox take off Kat Howard's cousin—may he rot and stink through the earth above his grave. He would not fight with me, but aboard a ship when I was sick set a Lincolnshire logget to beat me, a gentleman's son!'

'Why, thy gentility shall survive it,' Throckmorton said. 'But an it will not have more beating to its back, ye shall tell me where ye left T. Culpepper.'

'At Greenwich,' said the young Poins, and vomited forth curses. The old woman came from her pots to peer at the plasters on his skull, and then returned to the fire gibbering and wailing that she was not in that house plasters for to make.

'Knave,' Throckmorton said, 'an ye will not tell me your tale swiftly ye shall right now to the Tower. It is life and death to a leaden counter an I find not Culpepper ere nightfall.'

The young Poins stretched forth his arm and groaned.

'Part is bruises and part is sickness of the waves,' he muttered; 'but if I make not shift to slit his weazand ere nightfall, pox take all my advancement for ever. I will tell my weary tale.'

Throckmorton paused, held his head down, fingered his beard, and said:

'When left ye him at Greenwich?'

'This day at dawn,' Poins answered, and cursed again.

'Drunk or sober?'

'Drunk as a channel codfish.'

The old woman came, a sheaf of jack-knives in her arms, muttering along the table.

'Get you to bed,' she croaked. 'I will not ha' warmed new sheets for thee, and thee not use them. Get thee to bed.'

Throckmorton pushed her back, and caught the boy by the jacket near the throat.

'Ye shall tell me the tale as we go,' he said, and punctuated his words by shakes. 'But, oaf that I trusted to do a man's work, ye swing beneath a tree this night an we find not the man ye failed to stay.'

The young Poins—he panted out the story as he trotted, wofully keeping pace to Throckmorton's great strides between the hedges—had stuck to Culpepper as to his shadow, in Calais town. At each turn he had showed the warrant to be master of the lighters; he had handed over the gold that Throckmorton had given him. But Culpepper had turned a deaf ear to him, and, setting up a violent friendship with the Lincolnshire gatewarden over pots of beer in a brewhouse, had insisted on buying Hogben out of his company and taking him over the sea to be witness of his wedding with Katharine Howard. Dogged, and thrusting his word and his papers in at every turn, the young Poins had pursued them aboard a ship bound for the Thames.

This story came out in jerks and with divagations, but it was evident to Throckmorton that the young man had stuck to his task with a dogged obtuseness enough to have given offence to a dozen Culpeppers. He had begged him, in the inn, to take the lieutenancy of the Calais lighters; he had trotted at Culpepper's elbow in the winding streets; he had stood in his very path on the gangway to the ship that was to take them to Greenwich. At every step he had pulled out of his poke the commission for the lieutenancy—so that Throckmorton had in his mind, by the time they sat in the stern of the swift barge, the image of Culpepper as a savage bulldog pursued along streets and up ship-sides by a gambolling bear cub that pulled at his ears and danced before him. And he could credit Culpepper only with a saturnine and drunken good humour at having very successfully driven Cardinal Pole out of Paris. That was the only way in which he could account for the fact that Culpepper had not spitted the boy at the first onslaught. But for the sheer ill-luck of his sword's having been stolen, he might have done it, and been laid by the heels for six months in Calais. For Calais being a frontier town of the English realm, it was an offence very serious there for English to draw sword upon English, however molested.

It was that upon which Throckmorton had counted; and he cursed the day when Culpepper had entered the thieves' hut outside Ardres. But for that Culpepper must have drawn upon the boy; he must have been lying then in irons in Calais holdfast. As it was, there was this long chase. God knew whether they would find him in Greenwich; God knew where they would find him. He had gone to Greenwich, doubtless, because when he had left England the Court had been in Greenwich, and he expected there to find his cousin Kat. He would fly to Hampton as soon as he knew she was at Hampton; but how soon would he know it? By Poins' account, he was too drunk to stand, and had been carried ashore on the back of his Lincolnshire henchman. Therefore he might be lying in the streets of Greenwich—and Greenwich was a small place. But different men carried their liquor so differently, and Culpepper might go ashore too drunk to stand and yet reach Hampton sober enow to be like a raging bear by eventide.

That above all things Throckmorton dreaded. For that evening Katharine would be come back from the interview with Anne of Cleves at Windsor; and whether she had succeeded or not with her quest, the King was certain to be with her in her room—to rejoice on the one hand, or violently to plead his cause on the other. And Throckmorton knew his King well enough—he knew, that is to say, his private image of his King well enough—to be assured that a meeting between the King then and Culpepper there, must lead Katharine to her death. He considered the blind, immense body of jealousy that the King was. And, at Hampton, Privy Seal would have all avenues open for Culpepper to come to his cousin. Privy Seal had detailed Viridus, who had had the matter all the while in hand, to inflame Culpepper's mind with jealousy so that he should run shouting through the Court with a monstrous outcry.

It was because of this that Throckmorton dreaded to await Culpepper at Hampton; there he was sure enow to find him, sooner or later, but there would be the many spies of Privy Seal's around all the avenues to the palace. He might himself send away the spies, but it was too dangerous; for, say what he would, if he held Culpepper from Katharine Howard, Cromwell would visit it mercilessly upon him.

He turned the nose of his barge down the broadening, shining grey stream towards Greenwich. The wind blew freshly up from the sea; the tide ran down, and Throckmorton pulled his bonnet over his eyes to shade them from sea and breeze, and the wind that the rowers made. For it was the swiftest barge of the kingdom: long, black, and narrow, with eight watermen rowing, eight to relieve them, and always eight held in reserve at all landing stages for that barge's crew. So well Privy Seal had organised even the mutinous men of the river that his service might be swift and sudden. Throckmorton had set down the bower at the stern, that the wind might have less hold.

Nevertheless it blew cold, and he borrowed a cloak and a pottle of sack to warm the young Poins, who had run with him capless and without a coat. For, listening to the boy's disjointed tale out in the broad reaches below London, Throckmorton recognised that if the young man were incredibly a fool he was incredibly steadfast too, and a steadfast fool is a good tool to retain for simple work. He had, too—the boy—a valuable hatred for Culpepper that he allowed to transfer itself to Katharine herself: a brooding hatred that hung in his blue eyes as he gazed downwards at the barge floor or spat at the planks of the side. Its ferocity was augmented by the patches of plaster that stretched over his skull and dropped over one blonde eyebrow.

'Cod!' he ejaculated. 'Cod! Cod! Cod!' and waved a fist ferociously at the rushes that spiked the waters of the river in their new green. 'They waited till I was too sick of the sickness of the sea, too sick to stand—more mortal sick than ever man was. I hung to a rope and might not let go. And Cod! Cod! Cod! Culpepper lay under the sterncastle in a hole and set his Lincolnshire beast to baste my ribs.'

He spat again with gloomy quiescence into the bottom of the boat.

'In the mid of the sea,' he said, 'where the ship pointed at heaven and then at the fiend his home, I hung to a rope and was basted! And that whore's son lay in his hole and laughed. For I was a cub, says he, and not fit for a man's converse or striking.'

Throckmorton's eyes glimmered a little.

'You have been used as befits no gentleman's son,' he said. 'I will see to the righting of your wrongs.'

Poins swore with an amazing obscenity.

'Shall right 'em myself,' he said, 'so I meet T. Culpepper in this flesh as a man.'

Throckmorton leaned gently forward and touched his arm.

'I will right thy wrongs,' he said, 'and see to thine advancement; for if in this service you ha' failed, yet ha' you been persistent and feal.' He dabbled one white hand in the water, 'Nevertheless,' he said slowly, 'I would have you consider that your service in this ends here.' He spoke still more slowly: 'I would have you to understand this. Aforetime I gave you certain instructions as to using your sword upon this Culpepper if you might not otherwise stay him.' He held up one finger. 'Now mark; your commission is ceased. You shall no longer for my service draw sword, knife or dagger, stave nor club, upon this man.'

Poins looked at him with gloomy surprise that was changing swiftly to hot rage.

'I am under oath to a certain one to use no violence upon this man,' Throckmorton said, 'and to encourage no other to do violence.'

Poins thrust his round, brick-red brow out like a turkey cock's from the boat cloak into Throckmorton's face.

'I am under no oath of yourn!' he shouted. Throckmorton shrugged his shoulders and wagged one finger at him. 'No oath o' yourn!' the boy repeated. 'God knows who ye be or why it is so. But I ha' heard ye ha' my neck in a noose; I ha' heard ye be dangerous. Yet, before God, I swear in your teeth that if I meet this man to his face, or come upon his filthy back, drunk, awake, asleep, I will run him through the belly and send his soul to hell. He had me, a gentleman's son, basted by a hind!'

This long speech exhausted his breath, and he fell back panting.

'I had as soon ye had my head as not,' he muttered desperately, 'since I have been basted.'

'Why,' Throckmorton answered, 'for your private troubles, I know naught of them. There may be some that will thank ye or advance ye for spitting of this gallant. But I am not one of them. Nevertheless will I be your friend, whom ye would have served better an ye could.'

He smiled in his inward manner and went to polishing of his nails. A little later he felt the bruises on the boy's arms, and stayed the barge for a moment the stage where, swiftly, eight oarsmen took the places of the eight that had rowed two shifts out of three—stayed the barge for time enough to purchase for the boy a ham, a little ginger, some raw eggs and sack.

The barge rushed forward, with the jar of oars and the sound, like satin tearing, of the water at the bows, across the ruffled reaches of the broad waters. The gilded roofs, the gabled fronts of the palace at Greenwich called Placentia, winked in the fresh sunlight. Throckmorton had a great fever of excitement, but having sworn to let his oarsmen be scourged with leathern thongs if they made no more efforts, he lay back upon the purple cushions and toyed with the strings of the yellow ensign that floated behind them. It was his purpose to put heart in the boy and to feed his rage, so that alternately he promised to give him the warding of the Queen's door—a notable advancement—or assented to the lad's gloom when he said that he was fit only for the stables, having been beaten by a groom. So that at the quay the boy sprang forth mightily, swaying the boat behind him. The trace of his sea-sickness had left him; he swore to tear Culpepper's throat apart as if it had been capon flesh.

Throckmorton swiftly quartered the gardens, sending, in his passage beneath the tall palace arch, a dozen men to search all the paths for any drunkards that might there lie hidden. He sent the young Poins to search the three alehouses of the village where seamen new landed sat to drink. But, having found the sergeant of void palaces asleep in a small cell at the house end, he learned that two men, speaking Lincolnshire, had been there two hours agone, questing for Master Viridus and swearing that they had rid France of the devil and were to be made great lords for it. The sergeant, an old, corpulent Spaniard who had been in England forty years, having come with the dead Queen Katharine and been given this honourable post because the queen had loved him, folded his fat hands across his round stomach as he sat on the floor, his legs stretched out, his head against the hangings.

'I might not make out if they were lords or what manner of cavaliers,' he said. 'They sought some woman whom they would not name, and ran through a score of empty rooms. God knows whither they went.'

He pulled his nightcap further over his head, nodded at Throckmorton, and resumed his meditations.

There was no finding them in the still and empty corridors of the palace; but at the gateway he heard that the two men had clamoured to know where they might purchase raw shinbone of beef, and had been directed to the house of a widow Emden. There Throckmorton found their tracks, for the sacking that covered the window-holes was burst outwards, beef-bones lay on the road before the door, and, within, the widow, black, begrimed and very drunk, lay inverted on the clay of the floor, her head beneath the three legs of the chopping block, so that she was as if in a pillory, but too fuddled to do more than wave her legs. A prentice who crouched, with a broken head, in a corner of the filthy room, said that a man from Lincolnshire, all in Lincoln green, with a red beard, had wrought this ruin of beef-bones that he had cast through the windows, and had then comforted the screaming widow with much strong drink from a black bottle. They had wanted raw beef to make them valiant against some wedding, and they threw the beef-bones through the sacking because they said the place stunk villainously. They seemed, these two, to have visited every hovel in the damp and squalid village that lay before the palace gates. They had kicked beds of straw over the floors, thrown crocks at the pigs, melted pewter plates in the fires.

For pure joy at being afoot and ashore in England again, they had cast coins into all the houses and hovels of mud; they had brought out cans and casks from the alehouses, and cast pies into the streets, and caused the dismal ward to cry out: 'God save free Englishmen!' 'Curse the sea!' and 'A plague of Frenchmen that be devils!'

And the after effects of their carnival menaced Throckmorton, for from the miserable huts, where ragged women were rearranging the scattered straws and wiping egg-yolk from the broken benches, there issued a ragged crowd of men with tangled and muddy hair and boys unclothed save for sacks that whistled about their lean hips. The liquor that Culpepper and Hogben had distributed had rendered them curious or full of mutiny and discontent, and they surrounded Throckmorton's brilliant figure in its purple velvet, with the gold neck-chains and the jewelled hat, and some of them asked for money, and some called him 'Frenchman,' and some knew him for a spy, and some caught up stones and jawbones furtively to cast at him.

But, arrogant and with his head set high, he borrowed a whip from a packman that shouldered his way through the street, and lashed at their legs and ragged heads. The crowd slunk, one by one, back under the darkness that was beneath the roofs of reeds, and the idea of a good day that for a moment had risen in their minds at Culpepper's legendary approach, sank down and flickered out once more in their hungry bellies and fever-dimmed minds.

'God!' he said, 'we will have hangmen here,' and pursued his search. He met the young Poins at the head of the village street, and learned from him that Culpepper and his supporter had hired horses to ride to Hampton and had galloped away three hours before, holding legs of mutton by the feet and using them for cudgels to beat their horses.

'Before God!' the boy said, 'an I had money to hire horses I would overtake them, if I overtook not the devil erstwhile.'

Throckmorton pulled out his purple purse that was embroidered with silk crosses. He extracted from it four crowns of gold.

'Lad,' he said, 'I do not give thee gold to follow Kat Howard's cousin with. This is thy wage for the service thou hast done aforetime.' He reflected for a moment. 'If thou wilt have a horse—but I urge it not—to go to Hampton where thy fellows of the guard are—for, having served well ye may once more and without danger rejoin your mates—if ye will have such a horse, go to the horseward of the palace and say I sent you. Withouten doubt ye are mad to hasten back to your mates, a commendable desire. And the King's horses shall hasten faster than any hired horse—so that ye may easily overtake a man that hath but two hours' start towards Hampton.'

Whilst Poins was already hastening towards the gateway, Throckmorton cried to him at a distance:

'Ask at each cross-road guard-house and at all ferries and bridges if some have passed that way; and at the landing-stage if perchance caballeros have altered their desires and had it in their minds to take to boats.'

He sped through the wind to the riverside, set again his oars in motion and swept up the tide. It had turned and they made good progress.

VI

The Queen sat in her painted gallery at Richmond, and all around her her maids sewed and span. The gallery was long; along the panels that faced the windows were angels painted in red and blue and gold, and in the three centre squares St. George, whose face was the face of the King's Highness, in one issued from a yellow city upon a green plain; in one with a cherry-coloured lance slew a green dragon from whose mouth issued orange-coloured flames; and in one carried away, that he might wed her in a rose-coloured tower on a hillside, a princess in a black gown with hair painted of real gold.

Whilst the maids sewed in silence the Queen sat still upon a stool. Light-skinned, not very stout, with a smooth oval face, she had laid her folded hands on the gold and pearl embroidery of her lap and gazed away into the distance, thinking. She sat so still that not even the lawn tips of her wide hood with its invisible, minute sewings of white, quivered. Her gown was of cloth of gold, but since her being in England she had learned to wear a train, and in its folds on the ground slept a small Italian greyhound. About her neck she had a partelet set with green jewels and with pearls. Her maids sewed; the spinning-wheels ate away the braided flax from the spindles, and the sunlight poured down through the high windows. She was a very fair woman then, and many that had seen her there sit had marvelled of the King's disfavour for her; but she was accounted wondrous still, sitting thus by the hour with the little hounds in the folds of her dress. Only her eyes with their half-closed lids gave to her lost gaze the appearance of a humour and irony that she never was heard to voice.

They turned to the opening door, a flush came into her face, spread slowly down her white neck and was lost in the white opening of her shoulder-pieces, and she greeted Katharine Howard, kneeling at her feet, with an inclination of the head so tiny that you could not see the motion. Her eyes remained motionlessly upon the girl's face; only the lids moved suddenly when Katharine spoke to her in German.

'You speak my tongue?' the Queen asked, motionless still and speaking very low. Katharine remained upon her knees.

'I learned to read books in German when I was a child,' Katharine said; 'and since you came I have spoken an hour a day with a German astronomer that I might give you pleasure if so be it chanced.'

'So it is well,' the Queen said. 'Not many have so done.'

'God has endowed me with an ease of tongues,' Katharine answered; 'many others would have ventured it for your Grace's pleasure. But your tongue is a hard tongue.'

'I have needed to learn hard sentences in yours,' the Queen said, 'and have had many masters many hours of the day. I will have you stand up upon your feet.'

Katharine remained upon her knees.

'I will have you stand up upon your feet,' the Queen repeated.

'I have a prayer to make,' Katharine answered.

The Queen looked for a minute straight before her, then slowly turned her head to one side. When her gaze rested upon her women they rose and, with a clatter of their feet and a rustle of garments, carrying their white sewings and their spinning-wheels stilled, went away down the gallery. The German lord of Overstein, bearded and immense in the then German fashion, came from behind the retreating women to stand before the Queen signifying that he would offer his interpretership. She dismissed him without speaking, letting her eyes rest upon him. She was the most silent woman in the world, but all people said that no queen had women and men servers that needed fewer words or so discreetly did their devoirs.

The silence and the bright light of the sun swathed these two women's figures, so that Katharine seemed to hear the flutter against the window-glass of a brown butterfly that, having sheltered in the hall all winter, now sought to take a part in the new brightness of the world. Katharine kept her knees, her eyes upon the floor; the Queen, motionless and soft, let her eyes rest upon Katharine's hood. From time to time they travelled to her face, to the medallion that hung from her neck, and to her dark green skirt of velvet that lay around her upon the floor. The butterfly sought another window; the Queen spoke at last.

'You seek my queenship'; and in her still voice there was neither passion, nor pity, nor question, nor resignation.

Katharine raised her eyes: they saw the imprisoned butterfly, but she found no words.

'You have more courage than I,' the Queen said.

Suddenly she made a single gesture with her hands, as if she swept something from her lap: some invisible dust—and that was all. Still Katharine did not move nor speak; she had prepared speeches—speeches against the Queen's being disdainful, enraged, or dissolved in tears. She had read in books all night from Aulus Gellius to Cicero to get wisdom. But here there were no speeches called for; no speeches could be made. The significance of the Queen's gesture of sweeping dust from her lap slowly overwhelmed her.

'You have more courage than I,' the Queen repeated, as though slowly she were making a catalogue of Katharine's qualities to set dispassionately against her own; and again her eyes moved over Katharine. With her first swift gesture she drew from the stool-top a pamphlet of writing, upon which she had sat. Her face grew slowly red.

'It did not need this long writing against my person,' she said. 'I take it grievously.'

Katharine moved upon her knees as if she had been stung by an intolerable accusation.

'Before God!——' she began to say.

'Well, I believe you had no part in the writing,' the Queen interrupted her. 'Yet the more I say you have courage: to wed a man that will write lies of another woman's body and powers.'

Katharine sat still; the Queen's slow anger faded slowly away.

'I do not see why this King thinks you more fair than I be,' she said dispassionately; 'but what draweth the love of man to woman is not yet known.'

Again she repeated:

'There was no need of this writing against me. The King has never played the husband's part to me; I would have you tell him, if I go in danger from him, that, for me, he may go his ways. I have no mind to stay him, nor to be a queen in this country. Here, it is said, they slay queens.'

'If I will be Queen, it is that God may bless this realm and King with the old faith again,' Katharine said. Anne's eyelids narrowed.

'It is best known to yourself why you will be Queen,' she said. 'It is best known to God what faith he will have in this your realm. I know not what faith he liketh best, nor yet what side of a queen's functions most commendeth itself unto you.'

She seemed to withdraw herself more and more from any struggle, as if she were a novice that took an invisible veil—and she uttered only requests as to the world into which she would withdraw from this one.

'I am not minded to go back to Cleves,' she stipulated; for she had thought much and long in her stillnesses of what she would have; 'the Duke, my brother, is to blame for having brought me to this pass. Moreover, he is not able to defend his lands; so that if, with a proper establishing and revenue, I go back to Cleves, the Emperor Charles, who hath a tooth for gold, may too easily undo me. I would have a castle here in England; for England is an island, and well defended in all its avenues, and its King a man of honour and his word to such as never cross him, as never will I.'

She spoke slowly, as if in her mind she were ticking off little notes pencilled on her tablets; for since she could not read she had a memory that she could trust to. 'I will have a castle built me not strong enough to withstand the King's forces, since those I make no call to withstand, but strong enough to guard me against robber bands and the insurrections that are ordinary. Upon a slope that shall take the sun in winter, with trees about beneath which I may sit in the heat of summer-time. I will have a good show of servants, because I am a princess of noble lineage; I will have most of them Germans that I may speak easily with them, but some English, understanding German, so that the King may be advised I work no treasons against him. From time to time I will have the King to visit and to talk with me courteously and fairly as well he can: this in order to counterpart and destroy the report that I smell foul and am so ill to see that it makes a man ill——'

Her eyes, resting upon Katharine, closed slightly again with a tiny malice.

'I will have you not to fear that, upon such visits, I will use wiles to entrap the King. I do not favour him. I am not content to be queen of this country. It is as fair as my own country. In summer it is more cool, in the winter time more temperate. Meats here are good; cooks are better than with us. What a woman and a princess in this world would have is here all at the best, save only its men, and the most dangerous of all its men is the King.'

Katharine's ready anger rose at her words, though before the Queen's speeches had flowed above her head and left her speechless and ashamed.

'The King is known throughout Christendom,' she said, 'for the royallest prince, the noblest speaker, the most princely horseman, the most munificent and the most learned in the law.'

'That he may be,' the Queen smiled faintly, 'to them that have never crossed him. It has been my ill-destiny so to do.'

'Madam,' Katharine cried out, 'never man was so crossed, ill-served, evilly-led, or betrayed. Ye may not mislike him if at times he be petulant. I do the more praise him for it.'

'Why, you do love him,' the Queen said. 'I have no cause so to do.'

Katharine caught at one of her hands.

'Your Grace,' she said, 'Queen and high potentate, this realm calleth out that some one person do lead the King aright. Before God, I think I do not seek powers or temporal crowns. Maybe it is sweet to sit in a painted gallery and be a queen, but I have very little considered it; only, here is a King that crieth for the peace of God, a people that clamoureth aloud to be led back to the ways of God, a land parched for rain, swept by gales of wind and pestilences, bewailing the lost favour of God, and the Holy Church devastated that standeth between God and the realm.' The Queen listened to her as if, having made her stipulations, she had no more personal interest in the matter and were listening to the tale of a journey. 'Before God!' Katharine said, 'if you were not a virgin for the King, or if the King have coerced you to forswearing yourself in this matter, I would not be the King's wife, but his concubine. Only, sore is his need of me; he hath sworn it many times, and I do believe it, that I best, if anyone may, may give him rest with my converse and lead him to peace. He hath sworn that never woman save I made him so clearly to see his path to goodness; and never woman save I, at convenient seasons, have made him so forget his many cares.'

'Why, you have still more courage than I had thought,' the Queen said, 'to take a man so dangerous upon so little assurance.' She moved the hand that Katharine touched in her lap neither forward nor away; but at last she said:

'I am neither of your country nor for it; neither of your faith nor against it. But, being here, here I do sojourn. I came not here of mine own will. Men have handled me as they would, as if I had been a doll. But, if I may have as much of the sun as shines, and as much of comfort as the realm affords its better sort, being a princess, and to be treated with some reverence, I care not if ye take King, crown, and commonalty, so ye leave me the ruling of my house and the freedom to wash my face how I will. I had as soon see England linked again with the Papists as the Schmalkaldners; I had as lief see the King married to you as another; I had as lief all men do what they will so they leave me to go my ways and feed me well.'

She looked again upon Katharine, and for the first time spoke as if she were addressing her:

'I make out that you are a woman with an itch to meddle at the righting of the world. There have been more men than women at the task, but such an one was I never. The King was never man of mine, nor should have been had I any say in the matter.' She half closed her eyes again. 'Doubtless had it been otherwise the King would have constrained me by threats and tortures to forswear myself. I am as I was when I came to Dover. As the King saw me so he left me. Yet do I maintain and avow it was rather because he feared alliance with my brother's party than for any foulness of my person.'

Katharine passed her hands over her eyes.

'I do feel myself a thief and a cozener,' she said.

'Ye be none,' the Queen said; 'ye take no more than what I least prize of this world. Had it not been thee it might have been a worse; for assuredly I was not made to foot it with this King.'

'Nevertheless——' Katharine began. But the Queen was no more content to listen to her.

'Ye are as some I have known,' she said; 'they scruple to take what they very much crave, though it hang ready to drop into their hands; because they much crave it, therefore they scruple.' She had a small golden bullet beneath her clasped hands, and she cast it into a basin of silver that stood on a tripod beside her skirts. At the silvery clash and roll of the ball's running sound on the metal, doors opened along the gallery, and servitors came in bearing Rhenish wine in glass flagons and, upon great salvers, cakes in the forms of hearts or twisted into true-love-knots of pastry.

Katharine noted these things as being worthy of imitation.

'It is no more to me,' the Queen said, 'to lose the other things to you than to lose to you the wine that you shall drink or a pile of cakes.' Nevertheless she left Katharine upon her knees till she had taken her cup, for it pleased her that her servitors should see her treated with due worship.

VII

It was noon of that day when Katharine Howard set out again from Richmond to ride back to Hampton Court; and at noon of that day Throckmorton's barge shot dangerously beneath London Bridge, hastening to Hampton Court. At noon Thomas Culpepper passed over London Bridge, because a great crowd pressed across it from the south going to see a burning at Smithfield; at noon, too, or five minutes later, the young Poins galloped furiously past the end of the bridge and did not cross over, but sped through Southwark towards Hampton Court. And at noon or thereabouts the King, dressed in green as a husbandman, sat on a log to await a gun-fire, in the forest that was near to Richmond river path opposite Isleworth. He had given to Katharine a paper that she was to deliver to the master gunner of Richmond Palace in case the Queen Anne did satisfy her that the marriage was no marriage. So that, when among the green glades where the great trees let down their branches near the sward and shewed little tips of tender green leaves, he heard three thuds come echoing, he sprang to his feet, and, smiting his great, green-clothed thigh, he cried out: 'Ha! I be young again!' He pulled to his lips the mouth of the English horn that was girdled across his shoulder and under his arm; he set his feet wide apart, filled his lungs with air, and blew a thin, clear call. At once there issued from brakes, thickets and glades the figures of men, dressed like the King in yeoman's green, bearing bows over their shoulders, horns at their elbows, or having straining dogs in their leashes.

'Ho!' the King said to his chief verderer, a man of sixty with a grey beard, but so that all others could hear; 'be it well understood that I will have you shew some ladies what make of thing it is to rule over jolly Englishmen.' He directed them how he would have them drive the deer at the end of the glade; he saw to the setting up of white wands of peeled willows and, taking from his yeoman-companion, that was the Earl of Surrey, his great bow, he shot a mighty shaft along the glade, to shew how far away he would have the deer to pass like swift ghosts between the aisles of the trees.

But the palace of Hampton lay deserted and given up to scullions, who lay in the sunlight and took their rare ease. For a great many lords that could shoot well with the bow were gone to play the yeoman with the King; and a great many that had sumptuous and gallant apparel were gone to join the ladies riding back from Richmond; and the King's whole council, together with many lords that were awful or reverend in their appearance, were gone to sit in the scaffold to see the burning of the friar that had denied the King's supremacy of the Church and the burnings of the six Protestants that had denied the presence of Christ's body in the Sacrament. Only Privy Seal, who had ordered these things, was still walking in his gallery where he so often had walked of late.

He had with him Wriothesley, whose face was utterly downcast and abashed; he walked turning more swiftly than had been his wont ever before. Wriothesley hung down his great bearded, honest head and sighed three times.

'Sir,' he said at last, 'I see before us nothing but that ye make to divorce the Queen Anne.' And the words seemed to come from him as if they cost him his heart's blood.

Cromwell paused before him, his hands behind his back, his feet apart.

'The weighty question,' he said, 'is this: Who hath betrayed me: of Udal; of the alewife that he should have had the papers of; or Throckmorton?'

He had that morning received from Cleves, in the letter of his agent there, the certain proof that the Duke had written to the Emperor Charles making an utter submission to save his land from ruin, and as utterly abjuring his alliance with the King his brother-in-law and with the Schmalkaldner league and its Protestant princes. Cromwell had immediately called to him Wriothesley that was that day ordering the horses to take him back to Paris town. He had given him this news, which, if it were secret then, must in a month be made known to all the world. To Wriothesley the Protestant this blow was the falling in of the world; here was Protestantism at an end and dead. There remained nothing but to save the necks of some to carry on the faith to distant days. Therefore he had brought out his reluctant words to urge Privy Seal to the divorce of Anne of Cleves. There was no other way; there was no other issue. Privy Seal must abjure Cleves' Queen, and the very savour of a desire for a Protestant league.

But for Privy Seal the problem was not what to do, a thing he might settle in a minute's swift thought, but the discovery of who had betrayed him— for his whole life had been given to bringing together his machine of service. You might determine an alliance or a divorce between breath and breath; but the training of your instruments, the weeding out of them that had flaws in their fidelities; the exhibiting of a swift and awful vengeance upon mutineers—these were the things that called for thinking and long furrowing of brows. He considered of this point whilst Wriothesley spoke long and earnestly.

It was expedient before all things that Privy Seal keep the helm of the State; it was very certain that the King should not long keep to his marriage with the lady from Cleves; lamentable it was that Cleves had fallen away from Protestantism and from the league that so goodly had promised for truth in religion. But so, alas that the day had come! so it was. The King was a man brave and royal in his degree, but unstable, so that to keep him to Protestantism and good government a firm man was earnestly needed. There was none other man than Privy Seal. Let him consider earnestly that if it tasted ill with his conscience to move this divorce, yet elsewise such great ills should strike the kingdom, that far better it were to deaden his conscience than to sacrifice for a queen of doubtful faith the best hope that they had then, all of them, in the world. He spoke for many minutes in this strain, for twice the clock struck the half-hour from the tower above the gallery.

Finally, long-bearded, solemn, and richly attired as he was, Wriothesley went down upon one knee, and, laying his bonnet on the ground, stretched out a long hand.

'My lord,' he said, 'I do beseech you that you stay with us and succour us. We are a small band, but zealous and well-caparisoned. Bethink you that you put this land in peril if by maintaining this Queen ye do endanger your precious neck. For I were loath to take arms against the King's Majesty, and we are loyal and faithful subjects all; yet sooner than ye should fall——'

Cromwell stood over him, looking at him dispassionately, his hands still behind his back.

'Well, it is a great matter,' he uttered elusively. He moved as if to walk off, then suddenly turned upon his heel again. 'Ye do me more ill by speaking in that guise than ever Cleves or Gardiner or all my enemies have done. For assuredly if rumours of your words should reach the King when he was ill-affected, it should go hardly with me.'

He paused, and then spoke gently.

'And assuredly ye do me more wrong than ill,' he said. 'For this I swear to you, ye have heard evil enow of me to have believed some. But there is no man dare call me traitor in his heart of them that do know me. And this I tell you: I had rather die a thousand deaths than that ye should prop me up against the majesty and awe of government. By so doing ye might, at a hazard, save my life, but for certain ye would imperil that for which I have given my life.'

Again he paused and paced, and again came back in his traces to where Wriothesley knelt.

'Some danger there is for me,' he said, 'but I think it a very little one. The King knoweth too well how good a servant and how profitable I have been to him. I do think he will not cast me away to please a woman. Yet this is a very notable woman—ye wot of whom I speak; but I hope very soon to have one to my hand that shall utterly cast down and soil her in the eyes of the King's Highness.'

'Ye do think her unchaste?' Wriothesley asked. 'I have heard you say——'

'Knight,' Cromwell answered; 'what I think will not be revealed to-day nor to-morrow, but only at the Day of Judgment. Nevertheless, so do I love my master's cause that—if it peril mine own upon that awful occasion—I so will strive to tear this woman down.'

Wriothesley rose, stiff and angular.

'God keep the issue!' he said.

'Why, get you gone,' Cromwell said. 'But this I pray you gently: that ye restrain your fellows' tongues from speaking treason and heresy. Three of your friends, as you know, I must burn this day for such speakings; you, too—you yourself, too—I must burn if it come to that pass, or you shall die by the block. For I will have this land purged.' His cold eyes flamed dangerously for a minute. 'Fool!' he thundered, 'I will have this land purged of treasons and schisms. Get you gone before I advise further with myself of your haughty and stiff-necked speeches. For learn this: that before all creeds, and before all desires, and before all women, and before all men, standeth the good of this commonwealth, and state, and King, whose servant I be. Get you gone and report my words ere I come terribly among ye.'

Making his desultory pacings from end to end of the gallery, Cromwell considered that in that speech he had done a good morning's work, for assuredly these men put him in peril. More than one of these dangerous proclaimings of loyalty to him rather than to the King had come to his ears. They must be put an end to.

But this issue faded from his mind. Left to himself, he let his hands twitch as feverishly as they would. Cleves and its Duke had played him false! His sheet anchor was gone! There remained only, then, the device of proving to the King that Katharine Howard was a monster of unchastity. For so strong was the witness that he had gathered against her that he could not but try his Fate once more—to give the King, as so often he had done, proof of how diligently his minister fended for him and how requisite he was, as a man who had eyes in every corner of this realm.

To do that it was necessary that he should find her cousin; he had all the others under lock and key already in that palace. But her cousin—he must come soon or he would come too late!

Privy Seal was a man of immense labours, that carried him to burning his lamp into hours when all other men in land slept in their beds. And, at that date, he had a many letters to indite, because the choosing of burgesses for the Parliament was going forward, and he had ado in some burghs to make the citizens choose the men that he bade them have. He gave to each shire and burgh long thought and minute commands. He knew the mayor of each town, and had note-books telling him the opinions and deeds of every man that had freedom to elect all over England. And into each man he had instilled the terror of his vengeance. This needed anxious labours, and it was the measure of his concern that he stayed now from this work to meditate a full ten minutes upon this matter of bringing Thomas Culpepper before the King.

Thus, when, after he had for many hours been busy with his papers, Lascelles, the gentleman informer of the Archbishop's, came to tell him that he had seen Thomas Culpepper at Greenwich that dawn and had followed him to the burning at Smithfield, whence he had hastened to Hampton, the Lord Privy Seal took from his neck his own golden collar of knighthood and cast it over Lascelles' neck. In part this was because he had never before been so glad in his life, and in part because it was his policy to reward very richly them that did him a chance service.

'Sir,' he said, 'I grudge that ye be the Archbishop's man and not mine, so your judgment jumps with mine.'

And indeed Lascelles' judgment had jumped with Privy Seal's. He was the Archbishop's confidential gentleman; he swayed in many things the Archbishop's judgments. Yet in this one thing Cranmer had been too afraid to jump with him.

'To me,' Lascelles said, 'it appeared that the sole thing to be done was to strike at the esteem of the King for Kat Howard, and the sole method to strike at her was through her dealings with her cousin.'

'Sir,' Cromwell interrupted him, 'in this ye have hit upon mine own secret judgment that I had told to no man save my private servants.'

Lascelles bent his knee to acknowledge this great praise.

'Very gracious lord,' he said, 'his Grace of Canterbury opines rather that this woman must be propitiated. He hath sent her books to please her tickle fancy of erudition; he hath sent her Latin chronicles and Saxon to prove to her, if he may, that the English priesthood is older than that of Rome. He is minded to convince her if he may, or, if he may not, he plans to make submission to her, to commend her learning and in all things to flatter her—for she is very approachable by these channels, more than by any other.'

In short, as Lascelles made it appear to Cromwell's attentive brain, the Archbishop was, as always, anxious to run with the hare and hunt with the hounds. He was a schismatic bishop, appointed by the King and the King's creature, not the Bishop of Rome's. So that if with his high pen and his great gift of penning weighty sentences, he might bring Kat Howard to acknowledging him bishop and archbishop, he was ready so to do. If he must make submission to her judgment, he was ready so to do.

'Yet,' Lascelles concluded, 'I have urged him against these courses; or yet not against these courses, but to this other end in any case.' For it was certain that Kat Howard would have no truck with Cranmer. She would make him go on his knees to Rome and then she would burn him; or if she did not burn him she would make him end his days with a hair shirt in the cell of an anchorite. 'I hold it manifested,' Lascelles said, 'that this lady is such an one as will listen to no reason nor policy, neither will she palter, for whatever device, with them that have not lifelong paid lip-service to the arch-devil whose seat is in Rome.'

Cromwell nodded his head once more to commend the Archbishop's gentleman with a perfect acquiescence.

It had chanced that that morning Lascelles had gone to Greenwich to fetch for the Archbishop some books and tractates. The Archbishop was minded to lend them to the Bishop Hugh Latimer of Worcester; that day he was to dispute publicly with the friar Forest that was cast to be burned. And, coming to Greenwich, still thinking much upon Katharine Howard and her cousin, at the dawn, Lascelles had seen the tall, drunken, red-bearded man in green, with his squat, broad gossip in grey, come staggering up from the ship at the public quay.

'I did leave my burthen of books,' he said; 'for what be Bishop Hugh Latimer's arguments from a pulpit to a burning priest to the pulling down of this woman?' He had dogged Thomas Culpepper and his crony; he had seen him burst open windows, cast meat about in the mud and feed the populace of the Greenwich hamlet.

'And for sure,' he said, 'if the King's Highness should see this man's filthiness and foul demeanour, he will not be fain to feed after such a make of hound.'

Coming to Smithfield, where Culpepper stayed to cheer on the business, Lascelles had very swiftly begged the Archbishop, where, behind Hugh Larimer's pulpit, he sat to see Friar Forest corrected—had very swiftly begged the Archbishop to give him leave to come to Hampton.

'Sir,' Lascelles said, 'with a great sigh he gave me leave; for much he fears to have a hand in this matter.'

'Why, he shall have no hand,' Cromwell said. He clapped his hands, and told the blonde page-boy that appeared to send him very quickly Viridus, that had had this matter in his care.

Lascelles recounted shortly how he had set four men to watch Thomas Culpepper till he came to Hampton, and very swiftly to send word of when he came. Then the spy dropped his voice and pulled out a parchment from his bosom.

'Sir,' he said, 'whilst Culpepper was in the palace of Greenwich I made haste to go on board the ship that had brought him from Calais, being minded if I could to discover what was discoverable concerning his coming.'

He dropped his voice still further.

'Sir,' he began again, 'there be those in this realm, and maybe very close to your own person, that would have stayed his coming. For upon that ship lay a boy, sore sick of the sea and very beaten, by name Harry Poins. Wherefore, or at whose commands, he had done this I had no occasion to discover, since he lay like a sick dog and might not see nor hear nor speak; but this it was told me he had done: in every way he sought to let and hinder T. Culpepper's coming to England with so marked an importunity that at last Culpepper did set his crony to beat this boy.' He paused again. 'And this too I discovered, taking it from the boy's person, for in my avocations and service to his Grace, whom God preserve and honour! I have much practised these abstractions.'

Lascelles held the parchment, from which fell a seal like a drop of blood.

'Sir,' he said, 'this agreement is sealed with your own seal; it is from one Throckmorton in your service. It maketh this T. Culpepper lieutenant of barges and lighters in the town and port of Calais. It enjoineth upon him to stay diligently there and zealously to persevere in these duties.'

Cromwell neither started nor moved; he stood looking down at the floor for a minute space; then he held out his hand for the parchment, considered the seal and the subscription, let his eyes course over the lines of Throckmorton's handwriting that made a black patch on the surface soiled with sea-water and sweat, and uttered composedly:

'Why, it is well; it is monstrous well that you have saved this parchment from coming to evil hands.'

He rolled it neatly, placed it in his belt, and four times stamped his foot on the floor.

There came in at this signal, Viridus, the one of his secretaries that had first instructed Katharine Howard as to her demeanour. Since then, he had had among his duties the watching over Thomas Culpepper. Calm, furtive, with his thin hands clasped before him, the Sieur Viridus answered the swift, hard questions of his master. He was more attached and did more services to the Chancellor of the Augmentations, whom he kept mostly mindful of such farms and fields as Privy Seal intended should be given to benefit his particular friends and servants; for he had a mind that would hold many details of figures and directions.

Thus, he had sent two men to Calais and the road Paris-ward with injunctions to meet Thomas Culpepper and tell him tales of Katharine Howard's lewdness in the King's Court; to tell him, too, that the farms in Kent, promised him as a guerdon for ridding Paris of the Cardinal Pole, were deeded and signed to him, but that evil men sought to have them away.

'Ye sent no boy to stay him at Calais with lieutenancy of barges?' Cromwell asked, swiftly and hard in voice.

'No boy ne no man,' Viridus answered.

He had acted by the card of Privy Seal's injunctions; men were posted at Calais, at Dover, at Ashford, at Maidstone, at Sandwich, at Rochester, at Greenwich, at all the landing places of London. Each several one was instructed to tell Thomas Culpepper some new story that, if Culpepper were not already hastening to Hampton, should make him mend his paces. If he were hastening to Hampton they were to leave him be. All these things were done as Privy Seal had directed.

'What witnesses have ye here from Lincolnshire?' Cromwell asked.

In his monotonous sing-song Viridus named these people: Under lock and key in the King's cellary house, five from Stamford that had heard Culpepper swear Kat Howard was his leman—these had really heard this thing, and called for no priming; under instruction in the Well Ward gate chamber, four that should swear a certain boy was her child—these needed to have their tales evened as to the night the child was born, and how it had been brought from the Lord Edmund's house wrapped in a napkin. In his own pantry, Viridus had three under guard and admonition of his own— these should swear that whenas they served the Lord Edmund they had seen at several times Culpepper with her in thickets, or climbing to her window in the night, or at dawn coming away from her chamber door. These needed to be instructed as to all these things.

Cromwell listened with little nods, marking each item of these instructions.

'Listen now to me,' he said; 'give attentive ear.' Viridus dropped his eyes to the floor, as one who lends all his faculties to be subservient to his hearing.

'At six or thereabouts T. Culpepper shall reach this Court. Ye shall have men ready to bring him straightway to thee. At seven or thereabouts shall come the Lady Katharine to her room; with her shall come the King's Highness, habited as a yeoman. Be attentive. Next Katharine Howard's door is the door of the Lady Deedes. Her I have this day sent to other quarters. Having T. Culpepper with you, you shall go to this room of the Lady Deedes. You shall sit at the table with the door a little opened, so that ye may see when the King's Highness cometh. But you shall sit opposite T. Culpepper that he may not see.' Viridus remained like a statue carved of wood, motionless, his head inclined to the ground. Lascelles had his head forward, his mouth a little open. 'Whilst you wait you shall have with you the deeds giving to T. Culpepper his farms in Kent. These ye shall display to him. Ye shall dilate upon the goodness of the fields, upon the commodity in barns and oasthouses, upon the sweetness of the water wells, upon the goodliness of the air. But when the King shall be entered into the Lady Katharine's room you shall give T. Culpepper to drink of a certain flagon of wine that I shall give to you. When he hath drunk you shall begin to hint that all is ill with the lady he would wed; as thus you shall say: "Aye, your nest is well lined, but how of the bird?" And you shall talk of her having consorted much with a large yeoman. And when you shall observe him to be much heated with the subtle drug and your hintings, you shall say to him, "Lo, next this door is the door of the Lady Katharine. Go see if perchance she have not even now this yeoman with her."'

Viridus nodded his head once up and down; Lascelles clapped his hands twice for joy at this contrivance. Cromwell added further injunctions: that Viridus should have in the corner of the gallery a man that should come hastening to him, the Lord Privy Seal, where he walked in the gallery; another who, at his own signal, should hastily bring the witnesses prepared against Kat Howard; another who should bring the engrossment of a command to behead T. Culpepper that night in the King's Tower House, and yet another who should bring up guards and captains. All these, in their separate companies, should be set in the great room abovestairs next the King's chapel, so that they might swiftly and without hindrance or accident come down the little stair to the Lady Katharine's room. Again Viridus once bowed his head, moving his lips the while repeating these commands in words as they were uttered.

Cromwell paused again to think, then he added:

'I will set this gentleman, Lascelles, to bring T. Culpepper to you. And because I will make very certain that this man shall not touch the person of the King, I will have this gentleman to stay with you in the room where you be, to follow with you T. Culpepper into the Lady Katharine's room. He shall run with you betwixt T. Culpepper and the King; but if T. Culpepper be minded to fall upon the Lady Katharine, ye shall not either of you stay him. It were best if he might stab her dead. Doubtless he shall.'

'Before God!' Lascelles cried out, 'would I were a king to have so masterful and devising a minister as Privy Seal!'

'Get you gone,' Privy Seal said to Viridus. 'I ha' no need to tell you that if ye do faithfully and to a good issue carry out this play, you shall be greatly rewarded so that few shall hold their heads higher than you in the land. Ye know how I befriend my friends. But know too this: that if this scheme miscarry, either of your fault or another's, either through inattention or ill chance, either through treason or dullness of the brain of man, down to the least pin of it, ye shall not this night sleep in your bed, nor ever more shall you be seen in daylight above the earth.' He pointed suddenly from the window to the low sun. 'Have a care that ye so act as ye shall see that disc again!'

Viridus spoke no word, but having waited a minute to hear if Privy Seal had more to enjoin, noiselessly and with his hands folded before him as they had been when he came, moved away over the shining floor. He went to tell the old, shivering Chancellor of the Augmentations that he must absent himself upon their common master's errands. 'I misdoubt some heads will fall to-night,' he added as he went; 'our lord's nose for treasons is sharpened again.' And that creature of Privy Seal's shook beneath the furs that he wore, though it was already April; for the Chancellor had his private reasons to dread Privy Seal's outbursts of suspicion.

In the gallery, Privy Seal still spoke earnestly with Lascelles.

'I give this part of honour and privilege to thee,' he said; 'for though I was well prepared in all things, I trow I may trust thee better than another person.'

Lascelles was to watch for Culpepper, to hasten to Viridus, to attend upon the pair of them as the pilot-fish attendeth upon the ghostly and silent shark, not to leave them till the work was accomplished, or, upon the least sign of treason in Viridus or another, to come hastening as never man hastened, to Privy Seal.

'For,' Cromwell ended, 'ye have felt like me how, if this realm is to be saved, saved it shall be by this thing alone.'

Lascelles, who had had no opening to speak, opened now his lips. Great ferreter as he was, he had discovered former servants of the Duchess of Norfolk, that were ready, for consideration of threats, to swear that they had seen the Lady Katharine when a child in her grandmother's house to be over familiar with one Francis Dearham. He himself had these witnesses earmarked and attainable, and he was upon the point of offering them to Privy Seal. But he recollected that Privy Seal had witnesses enow of his own. To-morrow was also a day; and the King, if he would not now listen to tales against Kat Howard, might be brought to give ear to those and others added in a year's time, or when he began to tire of his woman as all men tire of women. Therefore he once more closed his lips. And Cromwell spoke as if his thoughts of a truth jumped together with Lascelles'.

'Sir,' he said, 'I would willingly bribe you from the service of his Grace of Canterbury to come into mine. But it may be that I shall not long outlive these days. Therefore I enjoin upon you these things: Serve well your master; guide him, for he needeth guidance, subtly as to-day ye would have guided him. I will not take you from him for this cause, that there is little need in one house of two that think alike. One sufficeth. For two houses with like minds are stronger than one that is bicephalous. Therefore serve you well Cranmer as in my day I served well the great Cardinal; so at his death, even as I at Wolsey's, ye may rise very high.'

He went swiftly into his little cabinet, and returning, had in his hand a little book.

'Read well in this,' he said, 'where much I have read. You shall see in it mine own annotations. This is "*Il Principe*" of Macchiavelli; there is none other book like it in the world. Study of it well: read it upon your walks. I am a simple man, yet hath it made me.'

Shadows were falling into the gallery, for the descending sun had come behind the dark, tall elms beyond the river.

'Upon my faith,' Cromwell said, 'and as I hope to enter into Paradise by the aid of Christ the King that commended faithful servants, I tell you I had great joy when you told me this woman's cousin had come into these parts. But greater joy than any were mine could I discern in this land a disciple that could carry on my work. As yet I have seen none; yet ponder well upon this book. God may work in thee, as in me, great changes by its study.... Get you gone.'

He continued long to pace the gallery, his hands behind his back, his cap pulled over his narrow eyes; it grew dusk so that his figure could scarce be seen where it was at the further end. He looked from the casement up into the moon, small and tenuous in the pale western skies. He had been going over in his mind the details of how he had commanded Culpepper to be brought before the King. And at the last when he considered again that Culpepper might well strike his cousin dead at his feet, and that then she would have no tongue to stand against calumnies withal, he uttered the words:

'I think I hold them.'

And, pondering upon the wonderful destiny that had brought him up from a trooper in Italy to these high places, he saluted the moon with his crooked forefinger—for the moon was the president at his birth.

'Why,' he uttered aloud, 'I have survived four queens' days.'

For Katharine of Aragon he had seen die; and Anne Boleyn had died on the scaffold; and Jane Seymour was dead in childbed; and now, with the news from Cleves, Anne's reign was over and done with.

'Four queens,' he repeated.

And, turning swiftly to the door, he commanded that Throckmorton be sent him at once when he came to the archway.

PART THREE
THE SUNBURST

I

In the great place of Smithfield, towards noon, Thomas Culpepper sat his horse on the outskirts of the crowd. By his side Hogben, the gatewarden, had much ado to hold his pikestaff across his horse's crupper in the thick of the people.

The pavement of heads filled the place—bare some of them, some of them covered, according as their owners had cast their caps on high for joy at the Bishop of Worcester's words against the Papist that was to be burned, or as they pressed their thumbs harder down in disfavour and waited to shew their joy at the hanging of the three Protestants that should follow. In the centre towered on high a great gallows from which depended a chain; and at the end of the chain, half-hidden by the people, but shewing his shoulders and his head, a man in a friar's cowl. And, towering as high as the gallows, painted green as to its coat and limbs, but gilt in the helmet and brandishing a great spear, was the image called David Darvel Gatheren that the Papist Welsh adored. This image had been brought there that, in its burning, it might consume the friar Forest. It gazed, red-cheeked and wooden, across the sunlight space at the pulpit of the Bishop of Worcester in his white cassock and black hat, waving his white arms and exhorting the man in the gallows to repent at the last moment. Some words of Latimer might now and again be heard; the chained friar stood upon the rungs of a ladder set against the gallows post; he hung down his head and shook it, but no word could be heard to come from his lips.

'Damnable heretic and foul traitor!' Latimer's urgings came across the sea of heads. 'Here sitteth his Majesty's council——' At these words went up a little buzz of question, but sufficient from all that great crowd to send as it were a wind that blew away the Bishop's words. For the style 'his Majesty' was so new to the land that people were questioning what new council this might be, or what lord's whose style they did not know. Latimer waved his arm behind him, half turning, to indicate the King's men. These ministers, bravely bonneted so that the jewels sparkled, habited in brown so that the red cloth covering their tiers of seats shewed between their arms and shoulders, sat, like a gay bank of flowers above the lake of heads, surrounded by many other lords and ladies in shining colours. They sat there ready to sign the pardon that was prepared if the friar would be moved by fear or by the Bishop's argument to hang his head and recant.

The friar, truly, hung his head, clung to the rungs of the ladder, trembled so that all men might see, and once caught furiously at the iron chain and shook it; but no word came from his lips. Culpepper was bursting with pride and satisfaction because he was a made man and would have all the world to know it. He swung his green bonnet round his red head and called for huzzays when the friar shewed fear. Hogben called for huzzays for Squahre Tom of Lincoln, and many men cheered. But the silence dropped again, and the Bishop's words, raised now very high, dominated the sunlight and eddied around the tall faces of the house fronts behind.

'Here have sat the nobles of the realm and the King's Majesty's most honourable council only to have granted pardon to you, wretched creature, if but some spark of repentance would have happened in ye.' Hanging his cowled poll beneath the beam that reached gigantic and black across the crowd, the friar shook his head slowly. 'Declared to you your errors I have,' cried Latimer. 'Openly and manifestly by the scriptures of God, with many and godly exhortations have I moved you to repentance. Yet will you neither hear nor speak——'

'Bones of St. Nairn!' Culpepper cried; 'here is too much speaking and no work. Huzzay! e caitiffs. Burn. Burn. Burn. For the honour of England.' And, starting from his figure at the verge of the crowd, cries went up of 'Huzzay!' of 'Burn!' and 'St George for London!' and unquiet rumours and struggles and waving in the crowd of heads, so that the Bishop's voice was not heard any more that day.

But through the crowd a silence fell as the image slowly and totteringly moved forward, ankle deep only in the crowd. Ropes from the figure's neck ran out and tightened—some among the crowd began to sing the song against Welsh Papists that ran—

'David Darvel GatherenAs sayeth the WelshmenFetched outlaws out of hell!'

and the burden of it rose so loud that the image swayed over and fell unheard. At that too a silence fell, and presently there came the sound of axes chopping. The friar, swaying on his ladder, looked down and then made a great sign of the cross. The Bishop in his pulpit, raising his white arms in horror and imprecation, seemed to be giving the signal for new uproars.

Whilst he shouted with delight, Culpepper felt a man catch at his leg. He kicked his foot loose, but his hand on the bridle was clutched. There was a fair man at his horse's shoulder that bore Privy Seal's lion badge upon his chest. His face was upturned, and in the clamour he spoke indistinguishable words. Culpepper struck towards the mouth with his fist; the man shrank back, but stood, nevertheless, close still in the crowd. When the silence fell again, Culpepper could hear amongst the swift chopping of the axes the words—

'I rede ye ride swiftly to Hampton. I am the Lord Cromwell's man.'

Culpepper brought his excited mind from the thought of the burning and the joy of the day, with its crowd and its odour of men, and sunshine and tumult.

'Ye say? Swine,' he shouted. 'Come aside!' He caught at the man's collar and kicked his horse and pulled at its jaws till it drew them out of the thin crowd to a street's opening.

'Sir,' the man said—he had a goodly cloth suit of dark green that spoke to his being of weight in some house-hold—'ye are like to lose your farms at Bromley an ye hasten not to Master Viridus, who holdeth the deedings to you.'

Culpepper uttered an inarticulate roar and smote his patient horse on the side of the head for two minutes of fierce blows, digging with his heels into the girthings.

'Sir,' the man said again, 'some lord will have these lands an ye come not to Hampton ere six of the clock. I know not the way of it that be a servant. But Master Viridus sent me with this message.'

Already a thin swirl of blue smoke was ascending past the friar's figure to the bright sky; it caressed the beam of the gallows and Culpepper's bloodshot eye pursued it upwards.

'Before God!' he muttered, 'I was set to see this burning. Ye have seen many; I never a one.' A new spasm of rage caught him: he dragged at his horse's head, and shouting, 'Gallop! gallop!' set off into the dark streets, his crony behind his back.

In the Poultry he knocked over a man in a red coat that had a gold chain about his neck; on the Chepe he jumped his horse across a pigman's booth—it brought down Hogben, horse and pike; three drunken men were fighting in Paternoster Street—Culpepper charged above their bodies; but very shortly he came through Temple Bar and was in the marshes and fields. Well out between the hedgerows he was aware that one galloped behind him. He drew a violent rein where the Cow Brook crossed the deep muddied road and looked back.

'Sir,' he called, 'this night I will hold a mouse on a chain above a coal fire. So I will see a burning, and my cousin Kat shall see it with me.' He spurred on again.

By the time he was come to Brentford four men, habited like the first, rode behind him. When he stayed to let his horse drink from the river opposite Richmond Hill, he was aware that across the stream a pageant with sweet music marched a little beyond the further bank. He could see the tops of pikes and pennons amid the tree trunks.

He muttered that such a pageant he would very soon make for himself; for, filled with the elation of his new magnificence, since Privy Seal was his friend and Viridus was earnest to do him favour, he imagined that no captain nor lord in that land soon should overpass him. For that any lord should desire his new lands troubled him little; only he hastened to cut that lord's throat and to kiss his cousin Kat.

It was a quarter before six when he drew rein in the green yard that lay before the King's arch in Hampton. There befel the strangest scuffle there; flaring for a moment and gone out like the gunpowder they sometimes lit in saucers for sport. A man called Lascelles came slowly from under the arch to meet him, and then, running over the green grass from the little side door, came the young Poins in red breeches, pulling off a red coat that he had had but half the time to don and tugging at his sword whose hilt was caught in the sleeve hole. Even as he issued, Lascelles, walking slowly, began to run and to call. Four other men of Privy Seal's ran from under the arch, and the four men that had followed behind him so far, closed their horses round his. The boy had his sword out and his coat gave as he ran. Lascelles closed near him on the grass, stretched out a foot to trip, and the boy lay sprawling, his hands stretched out, his sword three yards before him. The four men that had run from the arch had him up upon his feet and held his arms when Culpepper had ridden the hundred yards from the gate to them.

'Why,' said Culpepper, gazing upon the boy's face, 'it was thee wouldst have my farms.' He spat in the boy's face and rode complacently under the archway where were many men of Privy Seal's in the side chambers and on the steps that ran steeply to the King's new hall.

'I do conceive now,' Culpepper, in descending from his horse, spoke to Lascelles, 'wherefore that knave would have had me stay in Calais and be warder of barges. 'A would have my lands here.'

Word was given him that he must without delay go to the Sieur Viridus, and in a high good humour he followed the lead of Lascelles through the rabbit warren of small and new passages of the palace. In them it was already nearly dark.

It was in that way that, landing at the barge stage, a little stiff with the cold of his barge journey, Throckmorton came upon the young Poins in his scarlet breeches, his face cut and bleeding in his contact with the earth, his sword gone. Privy Seal's men that had fallen upon him had kicked him out of the palace gates. They had no warrant yet to take him; the quarrel was none of theirs. The boy was of the King's Guard, it was true, but his company lay then at the Tower.

Throckmorton cursed at him when he heard his news; and when he heard that Culpepper was then in the palace where window lights already shone before him, he ran to the archway. He had no time for reflection save as he ran. Word was given him in the archway itself that Privy Seal would see him instantly and with great haste and urgency. He asked only for news where Thomas Culpepper was, and ran, upon the disastrous hearing that Viridus had taken him up the privy stairway. And, in that darkness, thoughts ran in his head. Disaster was here. But what? Privy Seal called for him. He had no time for Privy Seal. Culpepper was gone to Kat Howard's room. Viridus there had taken him. There was no other room up the winding staircase to which he could go. Here was disaster! For whether he stayed Culpepper or no, Privy Seal must know that he had betrayed him. As he ran swiftly the desperate alternative coursed in his mind. Rich, the Chancellor of the Augmentations, and he had their tale pat, that Privy Seal was secretly raising the realm against the King. He himself had got good matter that morning listening to the treasonable talking of the printer Badge.

Several men in the stair angle would have stopped him when at last he was at foot of the winding stairs. He whispered:

'I be Throckmorton upon my master's business,' and was through and in the darkness of the stairway.

Why was there no cresset? Why were there these men? It came into his mind that already the King had heard Culpepper. Already Katharine was arrested. He groaned as he mounted the stairs. For in that case, with those men behind him, he was in a gaol already. He paused to go back; then it came to him that, if he could win forward and find the King, who alone, by giving ear, could save him, he would yet not know first how Katharine had fared. He had a great stabbing at his heart with that thought, and once more mounted.

From the door next hers there streamed a light. Hers was closed. He ran to it and knocked, leaning his head against the panels to listen. There was no sound, no sound at all when he knocked again. It was intolerable. He thrust the door open. No woman was there and no man. He went in. He thought: 'If the room be in disorder——'

He made out in the twilight that the room stood as always; the chair loomed where it should; there was a spark on the hearth; the books were ordered on the table; no stool was overturned. He stood amid these things, his heart beating tumultuously, his ears pricked up, stilling his breathing to listen, in the blue twilight, like a wild beast.

A voice said:

'Body o' God! Throckmorton!' beneath its breath, the light of the next door grew large and smaller again; he caught from there the words: 'It is Throckmorton.' And at the sound Throckmorton loosened his dagger in its sheath. Some glimmering of the plan reached him; they were awaiting Katharine's coming, and a great load fell from his mind. She was not yet taken.

He paused to stroke his beard for fear it was disordered, pulled from over his shoulder the medallion on the chain; it had flown there as he ran. He pushed ajar the next door a minute later, having thought many thoughts and appearing stately and calm.

He replaced the door at its exact angle and gazed at the three silent men. Thomas Culpepper, his brows knotted, his lips moving, was holding his head askew to see the measurements upon a map of his farm at Bromley. That Lascelles had gone out and come back saying that one Throckmorton was in the next room was nothing to him. The next room was nothing to him; he was there to hear of his farms.

Viridus, silent, dark and enigmatic, gazed at a spot upon the table; Lascelles, his mouth a little open, his eyes dilated, had his hands upon it.

Without speaking, Throckmorton noted that the room was empty save for the table and benches; the hangings had been taken down; all the furnishings were gone. That morning the room had been well filled, warm, and in the occupancy of the Lady Deedes. Therefore Cromwell had worked this change. No other had this power. They waited, then, those three, for the coming of Katharine Howard or the King. Lascelles shewed fear and surprise at his being there; therefore Lascelles was deeply concerned in this matter. Lascelles was in the service of Cranmer that morning; now he sat there. Thus he, too, for certain, was in this plan; he was a new servant to Privy Seal—and new servants are zealous. With Viridus he had had some talk of events. Therefore Lascelles was the greatest danger.

Throckmorton moved slowly behind Culpepper and sat down beside him; in his left hand he had his small dagger, its blue blade protruding from the ham; Culpepper beside him was at his right. He said very softly in Italian to Lascelles:

'Both your hands are upon the table; if you move one my dagger pierces your eye to the brain. So also if you speak in the English language.'

Lascelles muttered: 'Judas! *Traditore!* Viridus sat motionless, and Culpepper moved his finger across the plan of the farm.

'Here is the mixen,' he appealed to Viridus, who nodded.

It was as if Throckmorton, with his slow manner and low voice, was a friend who had come in to speak to Lascelles about the weather or the burnings. He was no concern of Culpepper's, nor was Lascelles who had spoken no word at all.

Throckmorton kept his head turned towards Lascelles as if he were still addressing him, and spoke in the same level voice, still in Italian.

'Viridus, to thee I speak. This is a very great matter.' Unconsciously he used the set form of words of Privy Seal. 'Consider well these things. The day of our master is nigh at an end. Rich, Chancellor of the Augmentations, thy crony and master, and my ally, hath made a plan to go with me to the King this night with witnesses and papers accusing Privy Seal of raising the land against his Highness. Will you join with us, or will you be lost with Privy Seal?'

Viridus kept his eyes upon the same spot of the table.

'Tell me more,' he said. 'This matter is very weighty.' His tone was level, monotonous and still. He too might have been saying that the sunshine that day had been long.

'A fad to talk Latin of ye courtiers,' Culpepper said with uninterested scorn. 'Ye will forget God's language of English.' He slapped Throckmorton on the sleeve. 'See, what a fine farm I have for my deserts,' he said.

'Ye shall have better,' Throckmorton said. 'I have moved the King in your behalf.' But he kept his eyes on Lascelles.

Culpepper cast back his cap from his eyes and leant away the better to slap Throckmorton on the back.

'Ye ha' heard o' my deeds,' he said.

'All England rings with them,' Throckmorton said. He interjected, 'Still! hound!' to Lascelles in Italian, and went on to Culpepper: 'I ha' moved the King to come this night to thy cousin's room hard by for I knew ye would go to her. The King is hot to speak with thee. Comport thyself as I do bid thee and art a made man indeed.'

Culpepper laughed with hysterical delight.

'By Cock!' he shouted. 'Master Viridus, thou art naught to this. Three farms shall not content me nor yet ten.'

Throckmorton's eyes shot a glance at Viridus and back again to Lascelles' face.

'If you speak I slay you,' he said. Lascelles' eyes started from his head, his mouth worked, and on the table his hands jerked convulsively. But Throckmorton had seen that Viridus still sat motionless.

'By Cock!' Culpepper cried. 'By Guy and Cock! let me kiss thee.'

'Sir,' Throckmorton said, 'I pray you speak no more words, not at all till I bid you speak. I am a very great lord here; you shall observe gravity and decorum or never will I bring you to the King. You are not made for Courts.'

'Oh, I kiss your hands,' Culpepper answered him. 'But wherefore have you a dagger?'

'Sir,' Throckmorton said again, 'I will have you silent, for if the King should pass the door he will be offended by your babble.' He interjected to Viridus, speaking in Italian, 'Speak thou to this fool and engage him to think. I can give you no more grounds, but you must quickly decide either to go with Rich the Chancellor and myself or to remain the liege of the Privy Seal.'

Never once did he take his eyes from Lascelles, and the sweat stood upon his forehead. Once when Lascelles moved he slid the dagger along the table with a sharp motion and a gasping of breath, as a pincer pressed to the death will make a faint. Yet his voice neither raised itself nor fell one shade.

'And if I will aid you in this, what reward do I get?' Viridus asked. He too spoke low and unmovedly, keeping his eyes upon the table.

'The one-half of my enrichments for five years, the one-half of those of the Chancellor, and my voice for you with the King and with the new Queen.'

'And if I will not go with you?'

'Then when the King passeth this door I do cry out "Treason! treason!" and you, I, and this man, and this shall to-night sleep in the King's prison, not in Privy Seal's. And I will have you think that I am sib and rib with Kat Howard who shall sway the King if her cousin be induced not to play the beast.'

Viridus spoke no word; but when Culpepper, idle and gaping, reached out his hand to take the black flagon of wine that was between them under the candles on the table, Viridus stretched forth his hand and clasped the bottle.

'It is not expedient that you drink,' he said.

'Why somever then?' Culpepper asked.

'That neither do you make a beast of yourself if you come before the King's great majesty this night,' Viridus said in his cold and minatory voice, 'not yet smell beastly of liquors when you kiss the King his hand.'

Culpepper said:

'By Cock! I had forgot the King's highness.'

'See that you kneel before him and speak not; see that you raise your eyes not from the floor nor breathe loudly; see that when the King's high and awful majesty dismisses you you go quietly.' Throckmorton spoke. 'See that you speak not with nor of your cousin. For so dreadful is a king, and this King more than others; and so terrible his wrath and desire of worship— and this King's more than others—that if ye speak above a whisper's sound, if ye act other than as a babe before its preceptor's rod, you are cast out utterly and undone. You shall never more have farms nor lands; you shall never more have joyance nor gladness; you shall rot forgotten in a hole as you had never done brave things for the King's grace.'

'By Cock!' Culpepper said, 'it seems it is easier to talk of a king than with one.'

'See that you remember it,' Throckmorton said, 'for with great trouble have I brought this King so far to talk with you!'

He moved his dagger yet nearer to Lascelles' form and held his finger to his lip. Viridus had never once moved; he stayed now as still as ever. Culpepper crammed his hand over his lips.

For from without there came the sound of voices and, in that dead silence, the rustle of a woman's gown, swishing and soft. A deep voice uttered heavily:

'Aye, I know your feelings. I have had my sadness.' It paused for a moment, and mouthed on: 'I can cap your Lucretius too with "*Usque adeo res humanas vis abdita*——"' It seemed that for a moment the speaker stayed before the door where all three held their breaths. 'I have read more of the Fathers, of late days, than of the writers profane.'

They heard the breathing of a heavy man who had mounted stairs. The voice sounded more faintly:

'Now you have naught further to think of than the goodly words of Ecclesiastes: "*Et cognovi quod non esset melius, nisi laetare et....*"' The voice died dead away with the closing of the door. And as a torch passed, Throckmorton knew that the King had waited there whilst light was being made in Katharine's room. He said softly to Viridus:

'Whilst I go unto them you shall hold this dagger against this fool's throat. We gain as many hours as we may hold him from blabbing to Privy Seal. And consider that we must bring to the King Rich and Udal and many other witnesses this night.'

'Throckmorton,' Viridus said, 'before thou goest thou shalt satisfy me of many things. I have not yet given myself into thy hands.'

II

A weary sadness had beset Katharine Howard ever since she had knelt before Anne of Cleves at Richmond, and it was of this the King had spoken outside the door whilst they had waited for light to be made.

All Anne's protesting that willingly she rendered up a distasteful crown could not make Katharine hugely glad with the manner of her own taking it. And, when a messenger, dressed as a yeoman in green, had come into the bright gallery to beg the Queen and that fair lady the Lady Katharine Howard to come a-riding side by side and witness the sports that certain poor yeomen made in the woods upon Thames-side, she felt a sinking in her heart that no Rhenish of the Queen's could relieve. She desired to be alone and to pray—or to be alone with Henry and speak out her heart and devise how they might atone to the Queen. But she must ride at the Queen's right hand with the Duke of Suffolk at her left. It was so between their captives that the Cæsars had ridden into Rome after the taking of barbaric kings. But she had waged no war.

She did not, in her heart, call shame upon the King; she knew him to be a heavy man with bitter sorrows who must in these violentnesses and brave shows find refuge and surcease; it was her province to endure and to find excuse for him. But to herself she quoted that phrase of Lucretius that the King again repeated: there was a hidden destiny that tamed the shows of the great; and she was the mutest of that throng that upon white horses, all with little flags flying and horns blowing, cantered to see the yeomen shoot. For the ladies and knights, avid of these things, loved above all good bowmanry and wagered with out-stretched hands for the marksmen that most they deemed to have skill or that usually seemed to enjoy the fortunate favours of chance and the winds.

But, being alone with the King—(for when the Queen rode back to Richmond the notable bowman in green walked, holding Katharine's stirrup, back to Hampton at her saddle-bow)—she could not stay herself from venting her griefs.

'*Et cognovi quod non esset melius nisi laetari et facere bene in vita sua*'—Henry finished his quotation when they were within her room. He sat himself down in her chair and stretched his legs apart; being tired with his long walk at her saddle bow, the more boisterous part of his great pleasure had left him. He was no more minded to slap his thigh, but he felt, as it was his favourite image of blessedness to desire, like a husbandman who sat beneath his vine and knew his harvesting prosper.

'Body of God!' he said, 'this is the best day of my life. There doth no cloud remain. Here is the sunburst. For Cleves hath cut himself adrift; I need have no more truck with Anne; you have no more cause nor power to bend yourself from me; to-morrow the Parliament meets, such a Parliament to do my will as never before met in a Republic; therefore I have no more need of Cromwell.' He snapped his thumb and finger as if he were throwing away a pinch of dust, and when she fell to her knees before his chair, placed his hand upon her head and, smiling, huge and indulgent, spoke on.

'This is such a day as seldom I have known since I was a child.' He leaned forward to stroke her dusky and golden hair and laid his hand upon her shoulder, his fingers touching her flushed cheek.

'On other days I have said with Horace, who is more to my taste than your Lucretius: "*That man is great and happy who at day's end may say: To-day I have lived, what of storms or black clouds on the morrow betide.*"'...

He crossed his great legs encased in green, set his heavy head to one side and, though he could see she was minded to pray to him, continued to speak like a man uttering of his memories.

'Such days as that of Horace I have known. But never yet such a day as to-day, which, good in itself, leadeth on to goodness and fair prospects for a certain morrow.' He smiled again. 'Why, I am no more an old man as I had thought to be. I have walked that far path beside thy horse.' It pleased him for two things: because he had walked with little fatigue and because he had been enabled to show her great and prodigal honour by so serving her for groom. 'This too I set to thy account as my good omen. And that thou art. No woman shall have such honours as thou in this land, save only the Mother of God.' And, after touching his green and jewelled bonnet, he cast it from his head on to the table.

'Sir,' she cried out, and clasping her hands uttered her words in anguish and haste. 'Great kings and lords upon their affiancing day have ever had the habit of granting their brides a boon or twain—as the conferring of the revenues of a province, or the pardoning of criminals.'

'Why, an thou come not to me to pardon Privy Seal——' he began.

'Sir,' she cut in on his words, 'I crave no pardon for Privy Seal; but let me speak my mind.'

He said tenderly:

'Art in the mood to talk! Talk on! for I know no way to hinder thee.'

'Sir,' she said, 'I ask thee no pardon for Privy Seal, neither his goods ne his life. I maintain this man hath well served thee and is no traitor; but since that he hath ground the faces of the poor, hath made thee to be hated by bringing of false witness, hath made the thirsty earth shrink from drinking of blood, hath cast down the Church—since that this man in this way hath brought peril upon the republic and upon the souls of poor and witless folk, this man hath wrought worse treasons than any that I wot of. If ye will adjudge him to die, I am no fool to say: No!'

Henry wrinkled his brows and said:

'Grinding the faces of the poor is in law no treason. Yet I may not slay him save upon the occasion of treason. I would a man would come to me that could prove him traitor.'

Kneeling before the King she grasped each of his knees with one of her hands.

'Sir,' she said, 'this is your occasion, none of mine. I would ye would reconcile it to your conscience so to act to him as I would have you, for his injustice to the poor and for his cogged oaths. But yet grant me this: to cog oaths for the downfall of Privy Seal upon the occasion of treason ye must have many other innocents implicated with him; such men as have had no idea, no suspicion, no breath of treason in their hearts. Grant me their lives. Sir, let me tell you a tale that I read in Seneca.' She moved her body nearer to him upon the floor, set her hands upon his two arms and gazed, beseeching and piteous, up into his face.

'Sir,' she said, 'you may read it in Seneca for yourself that upon the occasion of Cinna's treachery being made known to the Emperor Augustus, the Emperor lay at night debating this matter in his mind. For on the one side, says he in words like this: "*Shall I pardon this man after that he hath assailed my life, my life that I have preserved in so many battles by sea and by land, after I have stablished one single peace throughout the globe into all the corners thereof? Shall he go free who has considered with himself not only to slay me but to slay me when I offered sacrifice, ere its consummation, so that I may be damned as well as slain? Shall I pardon this man?*" And, upon the other side, the Emperor Augustus, lying in the black of the night, being a prince, even as thou art, prone to leniency, said such words as these: "*Why dost thou, Augustus, live, if it is of import to so many people that thou diest? Shall there never be an end to thy vengeance and thy punishments? Is thy single life of such worth that so much ruin shall for ever be wrought to preserve it?*"'

'Why, I have had these thoughts,' Henry said. 'Speak on. What did this Emperor that thought like me?'

'Sir,' Katharine continued, and now she had her hands upon his shoulders, 'the Empress Livia his wife lay beside him and was aware of these his night sweats and his anguishes. "*And the counsels of a woman; shall these be listened to?*" she spoke to him. "*Do thou in this what the Physicians follow when their accustomed recipes are of no avail to cure. They do try the contrary drugs. By severity thou hast never, sire, profited from the beginning to this very hour that is; Lepidus has followed to death Savidienus; Murena, Lepidus; Caepio followed Murena; Eynatius, Caepio. Commence to essay at this pass how clemency shall act in cure. Cinna is convicted: pardon him. Further to harm thee he hath no power, and it shall for ever redound to thy glory.*'"

She leaned upon him with all her weight, having her arms about his neck.

'Sir,' she said, 'the Emperor Augustus listened to his wife, and the days that followed are styled the Golden Age of Rome, he and the Empress having great glory.'

Henry scratched his head, holding his beard back from her face that lay upon his chest; she drew herself from him and once more laid her hands upon his knees. Her fair face was piteous and afraid; her lips trembled.

'Dear lord,' she began tremulously, 'I live in this world, and, great pity 'tis! I cannot but have seen how many have died by the block and faggots. Yet is there no end to this. Even to-day they have burnt upon the one part and the other. I do know thy occasions, thy trials, thy troubles. But think, sir, upon the Empress Livia. Cromwell being dead, find then a Cinna to pardon. Thou hast with thy great and princely endeavourings given a Roman peace to the world. Let now a Golden Age begin in this dear land.'

She rose to her feet and stretched out both her hands.

'These be the glories that I crave,' she said. 'I would have the glory of advising thee to this. Before God I would escape from being thy Queen if escape I might. I would live as the Sibyls that gave good counsel and lived in rocky cells in sackcloth. So would I fainer. But if you will have me, upon your oaths to me of this our affiancing, I beseech you to give me no jewels, neither the revenue of provinces for my dower. But grant it to me that in after ages men may conceive of me as of such a noble woman of Rome.'

Henry leaned forward and stroked first one knee and then the other.

'Why, I will pardon some,' he said. 'It had not need of so many words of thine. I am sick of slaughterings when you speak.' A haughty and challenging frown came into his face; his brows wrinkled furiously; he gazed at the opening door that moved half imperceptibly, slowly, in the half light, after the accustomed manner, so that one within might have time to cry out if a visitor was not welcome. For, for the most part, in those days, ladies set bolts across their doors.

Throckmorton stood there, blinking his eyes in the candle-light, and, slowly, he fell upon his knees.

'Majesty,' he said, 'I knew not.'

The King maintained a forbidding silence, his green bulk inert and dangerous.

'This lady's cousin,' Throckmorton pronounced his words slowly, 'is new come from France whence he hath driven out from Paris town the Cardinal Pole.'

The King lifted one hand from his thigh, and, heavily, let it fall again.

Throckmorton felt his way still further.

'This lady's cousin would speak with this lady in cousin-ship. He was set in my care by my lord Privy Seal. I have brought him thus far in safety. For some have made attacks upon him with swords.'

Katharine's hand went to her throat where she stood, tall and half turning from the King to Throckmorton. The word 'Wherefore?' came from her lips.

'Wherefore, I know not,' Throckmorton answered her steadily. His eyes shifted for a moment from the King and rested upon her face. 'But this I know, that I have him in my safe keeping.'

'Belike,' the King said, 'these swordsmen were friends of Pole.'

'Belike,' Throckmorton answered.

He fingered nonchalantly the rim of his cap that lay beside his knees.

'For his sake,' he said, 'it were well if your Grace, having rewarded him princely for this deed, should send him to a distant part, or to Edinbro' in the Kingdom of Scots, where need for men is to lie and observe.'

'Belike,' the King said. 'Get you gone.' But Throckmorton stayed there on his knees and the King uttered: 'Anan?'

'Majesty,' Throckmorton said, 'I would ye would see this man who is a poor, simple swordsman. He being ill made for courts I would have you reward him and send him from hence ere worse befall him.'

The King raised his brows.

'Ye love this man well,' he said.

'Here is too much beating about the bush,' burst from Katharine's lips. She stood, tall, winding her hands together, swaying a little and pale in the half light of the two candles. 'This cousin of mine loves me well or over well. This gentleman feareth that this cousin of mine shall cause disorders—for indeed he is of disordered intervals. Therefore, he will have you send him from this Court to a far land.'

'Why, this is a monstrous sensible gentleman,' Henry said. 'Let us see this yokel.' He had indeed a certain satisfaction at the interrupting, for with Katharine in her begging moods he was never certain that he must not grant her his shirt and go a penance to St Thomas' shrine.

Katharine stayed with her hand upon her heart, but when her cousin came his green figure in the doorway was stiff; he trembled to pass the sill, and looking never at her but at the King's shoes, he knelt him down in the centre of the floor. The words coming to her in the midst of anguishes and hot emotions, she said:

'Sire, this is my much-loved cousin, who hath bought me food and dress in my days of poverty, selling his very farms.'

Culpepper grunted over his shoulder:

'Hold thy tongue, cousin Kat. Ye know not that ye shall observe silence in the awful presence of kings.'

Henry threw his head back and laughed, whilst the chair creaked for a minute's space.

'Silence!' he said. 'Before God, silence! Have ye ever heard this lady's tongue?' He grew still and dreadful at the end of his mirth.

'Ye have done well,' he said. 'Give me your sword. I will knight you. I hear you are a poor man. I give you a knight's fee farm of a hundred pounds by the year. I hear you are a rough honest man. I had rather ye were about my nephew's courts than mine. Get you to Edinbro'.' He waved his hand to Throckmorton. 'See him disposed,' he said.

Culpepper uttered a sound of remonstrance. The King leaned forward in his seat and thundered:

'Get you gone. Be you this night thirty miles towards the Northland. I ha' heard ye ha' made brawls and broils here. See you be gone. By God, I am Harry of Windsor!'

He laid the heavy flat of the sword like a blow upon the green shoulders below him.

'Rise up, Sir Thomas Culpepper,' he said. 'Get you gone!'

Dazed and trembling still a little, Culpepper stuttered his way to the door. When he came by her Katharine cast her arms about his shoulder.

'Poor Tom,' she cried. 'Best it is for thee and me that thou goest. Here thou hast no place.' He shook his head like a man in a daze and was gone.

'Art too patient with the springald,' the King said.

He thundered 'Body of God!' again when he saw Throckmorton once more fall to his knees.

'Sire,' he said—and for the first time he faltered in his level tones—'a very great treason has come to my ken this day!'

'Holy altar fires!' the King growled, 'let your treasons wait. Here hath this lady been talking to me very reasonably of a golden age.'

'Sire,' Throckmorton said, and he leant one hand on the floor to support him. 'This is a very great treason of men arming to sustain Privy Seal against thee! I have seen it; with mine own eyes I have seen it in thy town of London.'

Katharine cried out, 'Ah!'

The King leapt to his feet.

'Ho, I will arm,' he said, and grew pale. For, with a sword in his hand or where fighting was, this King had middling little fear. But, even as the lion dreads a little mouse, so he feared secret rebellions.

'Sire,' Throckmorton said, and his face was towards Katharine as if he challenged her:

'This is the very truth of the very truth, I call upon what man will to gainsay me. This day I heard in the city of London, at the house of the printer, John Badge——' and he repeated the speech of the saturnine man—'that *"he would raise a thousand prentices and a thousand journeymen to shield Privy Seal from peril; that he could raise ten thousand citizens and ten thousand tenned again from the shires!"*'

Katharine kept her eyes upon Throckmorton who, knowing her power to sway the King, nodded gravely and looked into her eyes to assure her that these words were true.

But the King, upon his feet, marched towards the door.

'Let us arm my guard,' he said. 'I will play Nero to London town.'

Nevertheless Throckmorton kept his knees.

'Majesty,' he said, 'I have this man in my keeping.' And indeed, at his passing London Bridge he had sent men to take the printer and bring him to Hampton. 'I pray your pardon that I took him lacking your warrant, and Privy Seal's I dare not ask.'

The King stayed in his pacing.

'Thou art a jewel of a man,' he said. 'By Cock, I would I had many like thee.' And at the news that the head of this confederacy was taken his sudden fear fell. 'I will see this man. Bring him to me.'

'Sire,' Katharine said, 'we spoke even now of Cinna. Remember him!'

'Madam,' Throckmorton dared to speak. 'This is the man that hath printed broadsides against you. No man more hateth you in land or hath uttered more lewdnesses of your chastity.'

'The more I will have him pardoned,' Katharine said, 'that his Highness and all people may see how little I fear his lyings.'

Throckmorton shrugged his shoulders right up to his ears to signify that this was a very madness of Roman pardoning.

'God send you never rue it,' he said. 'Majesty,' he continued to the King, 'give me some safe conduct that for half-an-hour I may go about this palace unletted by men of Privy Seal's. For Privy Seal hath a mighty army of men to do his bidding and I am one man unaided. Give me half-an-hour's space and I will bring to you this captain of rebellion to your cabinet. And I will bring to you them that shall mightily and to the hilt against all countervail and denial prove that Privy Seal is a false and damnable traitor to thee and this goodly realm. So I swear: Throckmorton who am a trusty knight.'

He was not minded to utter before Katharine Howard the names of his other witnesses. For one of them was the Chancellor of the Augmentations, who was ready to swear that Cromwell, upon the barge when they went in the night from Rochester to Greenwich, had said that he would have the King down if he would not wed with Anne of Cleves. And he had Viridus to swear that Cromwell had said, before his armoury, to the Ambassador of the Schmalkaldners, that ne King, ne Emperor had such another armoury, yet were there twenty score great houses in England that had better, all ready to arm to defend the Protestant faith and Privy Seal. These things he was minded to lay before the King; but before Kat Howard he would not speak them. For, with her mad fury for truth and the letter of Truth that she had gained from reading Seneca till, he thought, her brains were turned, she would begin a wrangle with him. And he had no time to lose; for his ears were pricked up, even as he spoke, to catch any breaking of the silence from the next room where Viridus held Lascelles at the point of his dagger.

The King said:

'Go thou. If any man stay thee in going whithersoever thou wilt, say that thou beest upon my business; and woe betide them that stay thee if thou be not in my cabinet in the half of an hour with them ye speak of.'

Throckmorton rose stiffly to his feet; at the door he staggered for a moment, and closed his eyes. His cause was won; but he leant against the door-post and gazed at Katharine with a piteous and passionate glance, moving his fingers in his beard, as if he appealed to her in silence as with the eyes of a faithful hound, neither to judge him harshly nor to plead against him. This was the day of the most strain that ever was in his life.

And gazing back at him, Katharine's eyes were filled with pity, so sick he appeared to be.

'Body of God!' the King said in the silence that fell upon them. 'Now I hold Cromwell.'

Katharine cried out, 'Let me go; let me go; this is no world for me!'

He caught her masterfully in his arms.

'This is a golden world, and thou a golden Queen,' he said.

She held her head back from his lips, and struggled from him.

'I may not find any straightness here. I can see no clear way. Let me go.'

He took her again to him, and again she tore herself free.

'Listen to me,' she cried, 'listen to me! There have been broadsides printed against the truth of my body; there have been witnesses prepared against me. I will have you swear that you will read of these broadsides, and consider of these witnesses.'

'Before God,' he said, 'I will hang the printers, and slay the witnesses with my fist. I know how these things be made.' He shook his fist. 'I love thee so that were they true, and wert thou the woman of Sodom, I would have thee to my Queen!'

She cried out 'Ah!'

'Child,' he calmed himself, 'I will keep my hands from thee. But I would fain have the kisses of thy mouth.'

She went to lean upon her table, for her knees trembled.

'Let me speak,' she said.

'Why, none hinders,' he answered her kindly.

'I swear I do love thee, so that thy voice is as the blows of hammers upon iron to me,' she said. 'I may have little rest, save when I speak with thee, for that sustaineth thy servant. But I fear these days and ways. This is a very crooked riddle. So much I desire thee that I am tremulous to take thee. If it be a madness call it a madness, but grant me this!'

She looked at him distractedly, brushing her hands across her eyes.

'It feels within my heart that I must do a penance,' she said. 'I have been wishful to feel upon my brow the pressure of the great crown. Therefore, grant me this: that I may not feel it. And be this the penance!'

'Child,' he said, 'how may you be a Queen, and not crowned with pomp and state?'

'Majesty,' she faltered, 'to prepare myself against that high office I have been reading in chronicles of the lives of them that have been Queens of England. It was his Grace of Canterbury that sent me these books for another purpose. But there ye shall read—in Asser and the Saxon Chronicles—how that the old Queens of Saxondom, when that they were humble or were wives coming after the first, sat not upon the throne to be crowned and sacred, but—so it was with Judith that was stepmother to King Alfred, and with some others whose names in this hurry I may not discover nor remember in my mind—they were, upon some holidays, shewn to the people as being the King's wife.'

She hung her head.

'For that I am humble in truth before the world and before my mother Mary in Heaven, and for that I am not thy first Queen, but even thy fifth; so I would be shewn and never crowned.'

She leaned back against the table, supporting herself with her hands against its edges; her eyes piteously devoured his face.

'Why, child,' he said, 'so thou wilt be that fifth Queen; whether thou wilt be a Queen crowned or a Queen shewn, what care I?'

She no longer refused herself to his arms, for she had no more strength.

'Mary be judge between me and them that speak against me,' she said, 'I can no more hold out against my joy or longings.'

'Sha't wear a hair shirt,' he said tenderly. 'Sha't go in sackcloth. Sha't have enow to do praying for me and thee. But hast no need of prayers.' He lulled her in his arms, swaying on his feet. 'Hast a great tongue. Speakest many words. But art a very child. God send thee all the joy I purpose thee. And, an thou hast sins, weight me further down in hell therewith.'

The light of the candles threw their locked shadows along the wall and up the ceilings. Her head fell back, her eyes closed, so that she seemed to be dead and her listless hands were open in her skirts.

Milton Keynes UK
Ingram Content Group UK Ltd.
UKHW041539121024
449426UK00005B/376